CHINESE KNOTTING

CHINESE KNOTTING
An Illustrated Guide of 100⁺ Projects

By Cao Haimei

Translated by Kitty Lau

Better Link Press

Page 1
Fig. 1   The traditional Chinese knot ornaments adorn our lives in many ways. The picture presents auspicious charms, stylish bracelets, practical coasters, etc.

Page 2
Fig. 2   This red charm combines the sixteen-squared endless knot and Chinese character of blessing (*fu*, 福), bringing you prosperity.

Page 3
Fig. 3   This necklace "blessings in four seasons" comes with a six-squared endless knot in the center surrounded by four *ruyi* knots, decorated with a number of single button knots, silver charms and beads.

Below
Fig. 4   Combine the four-squared endless knot pendant with the snake knots and porcelain tube beads to form this prosperity necklace.

Right
Fig. 5   Add a four-squared endless knot above and bundles of pineapple knots below to make the carp ornament more magnificent.

Note: In Chapter Four of this book, "Dia." means diameter, "L" means length, and "W" means width.

This book is edited and designed by the Editorial Committee of *Cultural China* series

Text: Cao Haimei

Photographs: Lin Yuming (projects), Cao Haimei (knotting demonstration)

Model: Cao Haizhou

Translation: Kitty Lau

Cover Design: Wang Wei

Interior Design: Li Jing, Hu Bin (Yuan Yinchang Design Studio)

Editors: Wu Yuezhou, Yang Xiaohe

Editorial Director: Zhang Yicong

Senior Consultants: Sun Yong, Wu Ying, Yang Xinci

Managing Director and Publisher: Wang Youbu

ISBN: 978-1-60220-019-7

Address any comments about *Chinese Knotting: An Illustrated Guide of 100⁺ Projects* to:

Better Link Press
99 Park Ave
New York, NY 10016
USA

or

Shanghai Press and Publishing Development Company
F 7 Donghu Road, Shanghai, China (200031)
Email: comments_betterlinkpress@hotmail.com

Printed in China by Shanghai Donnelley Printing Co., Ltd.

1   3   5   7   9   10   8   6   4   2

CONTENTS

CONTENTS

Fig. 6 This dragonfly keychain accommodates both functional and decorative needs.

CONTENTS

Fig. 7 This bracelet integrates the alternate half hitches and silver lotus charms, enclosed with the extended sliding flat knots, to deliver peace and luck.

Fig. 8   Set a series of right half hitches around a ring with a silver lotus pendant in the middle and button knots above to create this auspicious charm.

PREFACE
CHINESE KNOTTING AND I

My relationship with Chinese knotting started since I was young. When I was 4 years old, my grandmother told me a story about the origins of Chinese characters. Out of my curiosity, I asked her how people recorded daily incidents before the invention of Chinese characters.

"Back then, people tied some knots on the ropes as a record," my grandma replied. "For big incidents, they tied big knots; for little things, they tied small ones."

Another question arose. "Knots are knots, no matter how big or small they are. How did they clearly associate with different implications?" I was in doubt.

This was my first encounter with Chinese knotting.

At the age of 6, I received a basic jump rope. It slid out from my hands easily even when I did easy jumps. So I asked my housemaid for help. With her great ingenuity, she tied a button knot on the rope end. All I had to do was grapping the knot with my little hand and the problem was solved. Not only was it practical but also beautiful. I liked it so much that I begged her to teach me how to make the knot and I created one on the other end. This was my first Chinese knotting.

My maid at that time was sixty and really good at needlework. She fabricated lots of clothes, shoes, and hats for me. She also made knot buttons to enhance my clothing. Whenever she worked, I would sit on her side, watch quietly, and get fascinated by her exquisite craftsmanship. Under the guidance of such a wonderful teacher, I learned the techniques of good-luck knot, Chinese lute knot, and some other Chinese knots.

Later on, I went to Beijing Institute of Art and Design (now College of Art and Design of Beijing University of Technology) and studied textile dyeing and fashion design. To encourage traditional arts and crafts, the institute introduced a weaving and knotting course. I, with no hesitation, joined the class and started to gather information regarding Chinese knotting. Even after graduation, I continued to collect and organize the history, development, and technical information of this traditional Chinese art.

After studying knotting for a long time, I discovered that most Chinese knots carry a remarkable implication. Different combinations of knots deliver different meanings. These are the answers to my childhood questions.

Through interlacing, a simple cord can be transformed to a beautiful craft with a meaningful message. Chinese knotting attracted me since I was little and so I have tied the knot with it.

Cao Haimei

Fig. 9 There is a big contrast between these two innovated knots: the red elaborated stone chime knot ornament and the pink knot rose.

CHAPTER ONE
GETTING TO KNOW CHINESE KNOTTING

Chinese knotting is a traditional Chinese handcraft of interlacing silk cords and other materials. It is an art with a lot of styles, patterns, and implications.

In the old days, Chinese knotting was a very common needlework that mothers passed onto their daughters. It was widespread and developed among the folks. Women used their skillful hands to create various knots for decorative purposes, such as buttons and belts as part of the fashion. They were also used in daily household objects, such as jade pendants, folding fan pendants, and sachets. In the royal palaces, the craftsmen designed more sophisticated knotting art pieces. Eventually, the art established by the royal artists integrated with the general folks and continued to develop, which led to the expansion of Chinese knotting.

Chinese knotting is part of Chinese daily life. It is a symbol of Chinese culture. Even now, Chinese knotting continues to grow and is integrated with different aspects of living.

1. The Origins of the Names

There are various Chinese knotting styles. To some people, the names are mysterious. After the painstaking research, we can group Chinese knotting in four different categories.

Category I: Figurative, which is derived from the real objects, such as double-coin knot, cloverleaf knot, auspicious cloud knot, etc.

Category II: Implicational, which has auspicious or symbolic meanings, such as good-luck knot, three-outer-loop double-coin knot (solemn knot), etc.

Category III: Functional, which is according to their practical functions, such as button knot, binding knot, etc.

Category IV: Compositional, which is further developed from the basic types to generate special characteristics, such as compound double-coin knot, compound good-luck knot.

Fig. 10   Prosperity knot hair pin.

2. Types of Knots

Chinese knotting can be classfied according to the forms.

Basic knots: The forms are more independent. Most of them have only one cord. Furthermore, basic knots can be divided into basic single knots and basic supplementary knots depending on their characteristics.

Modified knots: They are extended and transformed from the basic knots or combined with several basic knots. A lot of them are handed down from generation to generation with meaningful implications. Moreover, the modified knots can be further divided into modified single knots and traditional modified combination knots according to their characteristics.

Innovated knots: Recently, a lot of newly innovated knots have been created. The shapes are advanced with new concepts. They can be further divided into innovative decorative knots and innovative representational knots according to their characteristics.

Basic Single Knots

The shapes of basic single knots are symmetrical and beautiful. They can be used alone since the structures are complete and inseparable.

There are more than 15 types of basic single knots, e.g. double-coin knot, flat knot, button knot, good-luck knot, sauvastika knot, cross knot, double-connection knot, cloverleaf knot, two-outer-loop cloverleaf knot, round brocade knot, tassel knot, endless knot, plafond knot, creeper knot, and constellation knot.

Fig. 11   Basic single knots: (clockwise) tassel knot, constellation knot, plafond knot, sauvastika knot, button knot, endless knot, good-luck knot, round brocade knot.

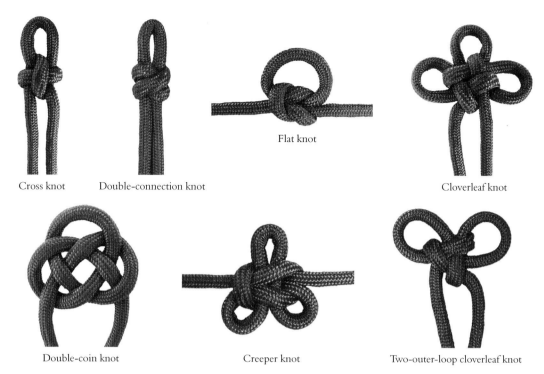

Flat knot

Cross knot   Double-connection knot   Cloverleaf knot

Double-coin knot   Creeper knot   Two-outer-loop cloverleaf knot

Fig. 12   Basic single knots

Basic Supplementary Knots

In general, the basic supplementary knots are smaller and required other elements to complete. They are usually combined with other knots or materials or interlaced with one another to be presentable.

There are more than 10 types of basic supplementary knots, e.g. binding knot (or lark's head knot), cross binding knot, overhand knot, left half hitch, right half hitch, multiple overhand knot, figure-eight knot, dew knot, sliding knot, and braid knot.

Fig. 14   These red and yellow knot crafts are composed of simple figure-eight knots and single figure-eight knots. Top: red bracelet with multiple overhand knots, sliding knot, and a colorful glass bead.

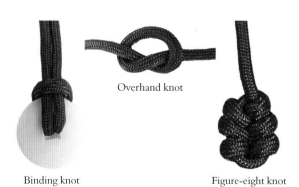

Overhand knot

Binding knot   Figure-eight knot

Fig. 13   Basic supplementary knots

Ruyi knot

Basket knot

Ten accord knot

Fig. 16 The blue-yellow-white coaster under the teacup is an example of basket knot.

Modified Single Knots
Modified single knots are based on the basic knots with modifications or they are combined with several basic knots to form new types of knots. It is common to be used alone.

Examples of common modified single knots are two-outer-loop double-coin knot, three-outer-loop double-coin knot, masthead knot, eleven-loop good-luck knot, stone chime knot, six-squared endless knot, eight-squared endless knot, cross endless knot, compound endless knot, compound round brocade knot, turtle shell knot, *ruyi* knot, basket knot, compound double-coin knot, prosperity knot, cage knot, ten accord knot, compound brocade knot, and *kasaya* knot.

Compound endless knot

Eleven-loop good-luck knot

Fig. 15 Modified single knots

Traditional Modified Combination Knots

Modified combination knots are typical traditional crafts. They can be a combination of basic knots, modified single knots, or basic knots with modified single knots. The goal is to bring forth auspicious implications by imitating the objects or using homophony.

Examples of common modified combination knots are double-diamond knot, Chinese lute button knot, *lingzhi* knot, butterfly knot, dragonfly knot, crane knot, phoenix knot, dragon knot, dharma-wheel knot, good-luck *ruyi* knot, blessings-in-four-season knot, halberd knot, longevity knot, happiness knot, double-happiness knot, spring knot, and prosperity knot.

Double-diamond knot: stone chime (top) & endless knot (bottom)

Butterfly knot: endless knot (center) & 2 double-coin knots (left & right)

Good-luck *ruyi* knot: good-luck knot (center) & 4 *ruyi* knots (top, bottom, left & right)

Fig. 18   The colors chosen for this set of knots are very harmonized and charming, which match the brown and blue coated pendant below.
Top to bottom: butterfly knot, eight-squared endless knot with tassels on both sides, button knot, binding knot.

Halberd knot: double-connection knots, cloverleaf knots, and two-outer-loop cloverleaf knots

Fig. 17   Traditional modified combination knots

Innovative Decorative Knots

Innovative decorative knots are transformed from the traditional Chinese knots with higher decorative intentions.

Examples of common innovative decorative knots are compound good-luck knot, horizontal plafond knot, endless good-luck knot, sauvastika creeper butterfly knot, compound constellation knot, twisted endless knot, compound cloverleaf knot, five-happiness knot, and six-unity knot.

Compound good-luck knot

Sauvastika creeper butterfly knot

Horizontal plafond knot

Fig. 19 Innovative decorative knots

Fig. 20 This horizontal plafond knot ornament with a porcelain bottle gourd charm and a tassel brings blessings and wealth.

Innovative Representational Knots

Innovative representational knots are created by imitating the actual plants, animals, or other objects.

The common innovated image knots are categorized as:

Ritual essentials, such as compound auspicious knot, good-luck prayer-wheel knot, good-luck *jingang* knot.

Plants, such as flowers, trees, fruits.

Animals, such as the twelve signs of Chinese zodiac, birds, fishes, insects.

Everyday goods: embroidered shoes, teapots, words, pianos, baskets.

Fig. 21   Innovative representational knot: good-luck prayer-wheel knot.

Fig. 22   Innovative representational knot: fish knot button.

Fig. 23 The overhand knot, binding knot, and cross binding knot are basic supplementary knots and yet they can be integrated together to form beautiful knot ornaments.

CHAPTER TWO
HISTORY AND DEVELOPMENT

Chinese knotting is seldom mentioned in historical records and relics. There are two main reasons. First, in folk arts, the technique was mainly passed on from mothers to daughters by word of mouth. Second, in royal palace, Chinese knotting was mainly used as a supplementary art for the artifacts; thus no official records had been found. Moreover, the materials used for knotting were usually perishable and most likely not able to persevere.

In order to find out more historical facts about Chinese knotting, we have to research from the antique paintings, sculptures, and artifacts.

1. The Origins

The use of knotting can be traced back to the Early Stone Age. Fishing and gathering edibles were the main sources of living. These encouraged the utilization of ropes for making nets and fastening foods, and became the origins of Chinese knotting.

About 20,000 years ago in the New Stone Age, people already used knotting for accessories (fig. 24). In the upper cave of Zhoukoudian, Beijing, some stone, bone, shell, and tooth accessories were found with marks of abrasion due to wearing for a long time. Among the hundred items, five were arranged in crescent shapes that were most likely to be connected in some sort. A needle was also found. As threads going through needles for sewing and binding accessories required knots to complete, this proved that functional knots were very popular at that time.

Fig. 24 A cluster of clam shells
Late New Stone Age
Excavated from Liyudi, Suixi, Zhanjiang, Guangdong
This clam shell accessory proves that knotting was practically used for binding in the New Stone Age.

Before the creation of writing system, knotting was used to keep records. *Zhouyi*, the *Book of Changes*, documented that there was no writing in the ancient times and people used knots to take notes and administer. After the invention of writing, knotting used for recording was abandoned. Since there was no paper, people engraved the scripts on potteries, bones or turtle shells. Zheng Xuan in the Han dynasty commented on the *Annotation of Zhouyi* that big knots were used to record big events while small knots were used to record small events.

Since the creation of writing, knotting for recording was dismissed. Instead, it is used for binding, and gradually for decorative purpose.

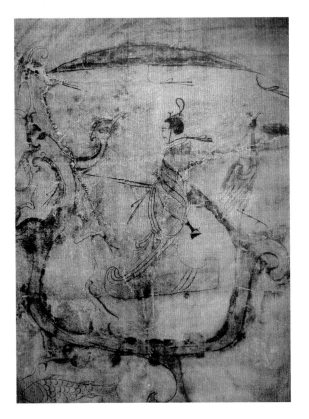

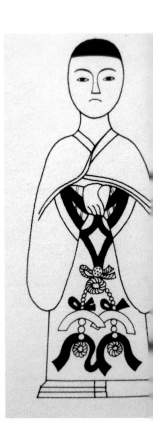

Fig. 25 *A Man Riding a Dragon*
The Era of Warring States (475–221 BC)
Excavated from No. 1 Chu Tomb in Zidanku, Changsha City, Hunan
Knots are found on the strings of the man's hat and canopy.

Fig. 26 Painted wooden figure line drawing copy
The Eastern Zhou dynasty (770–256 BC)
Excavated from No. 2 Chu Tomb in Changtaiguan, Xinyang City, Henan
This painted wood figure has a cluster of jades, which was popular at that time, at his waist. The cluster contains 3 parts, top, center, and the bottom. String is used to connect them together with the painted pendants.

2. From Function to Decoration

Since the Western Zhou dynasty (1046–771 BC), knots were commonly used in daily life, such as accessories on belts and canopies of carports (fig. 25). People in that period of time liked to tie up the seals on their belts. Buttons or eyes were found at all corners of the Han dynasty seals, which were obviously for hanging purpose so that they could be easily carried around as accessories. Hangers were also found at the back of the bronze mirrors. They were for the strings so that the mirrors became portable with decorations.

In the Western Zhou period, people in high status and scholars had to wear jade as per the etiquette. In the Zhou dynasty, jades represented the hierarchy and dignity. With such a big influence, both men and women in the upper class carried multiple jade accessories to prove their status. The jade accessories required strings to hang onto their clothes, especially for series of jades, which were connected by silk cords and knots (fig. 26).

Knotting can also been seen on ritual bronzes in the Era of Warring States (475–221 BC). Cord and knotting patterns are on the corded wares embedded by using the relief techniques. This confirms the popularity of knotting and application of decoration (fig. 27).

In this period, knots on clothing were the symbols of social status. The uniforms of the terracotta warriors of the Qin dynasty demonstrate the relationship between clothing and the hierarchy. The generals have prominent

Fig.27 Wares of Cord Patterns
The Era of Warring States (475–221 BC)
Shanxi Museum

Fig. 28 The General, Terracotta figure
(up right)
The Qin dynasty (221–206 BC)
Emperor Qinshihuang's Mausoleum Site
Museum, Xi'an City, Shaanxi

Fig. 29 The Archer, Terracotta figure (right)
The Qin dynasty (221–206 BC)
Emperor Qinshihuang's Mausoleum Site
Museum, Xi'an City, Shaanxi

Fig. 30 The portrait on the left door
of Qianliangtai Tomb
The Eastern Han dynasty (25–220)
Excavated from Qianliangtai Village,
Zhucheng City, Shangdong

knotting accessories on the chests and shoulders. The knots do not have practical functions but are used to show their ranking (fig. 28). The archers have large knotting accessories stretched from the shoulders to the chests, which are different from the generals (fig. 29). There are noticeable decorative knotting accessories on the uniforms of the Western Han dynasty guards to show the authorities and powers.

As shown on the relics, some basic knots used today had started to form in the Han dynasty. For example, the portrait on the left door found at Qianliangtai Mausoleum of the Eastern Han dynasty in Zhucheng City, Shandong, has the button knots on it (fig. 30). The red and yellow silk sachet discovered at the No. 15 cemetery in Yuli Yingpan, Xinjiang, comes with some very decorative three-outer-loop good-luck knots on the sides and floral knots on the wings and tail (fig. 31). The dragon painting on the lacquer coffin unearthed at the No. 1 Han Tomb in Mawangdui, Changsha City, Hunan, shows a suspended jade with knotted silk cords (fig. 32). From the same place, the painting of the *Assumption* illustrates two dragons flying through a piece of jade forming a cross binding knot. There were also tassels attached to the corners of the painting.

Fig. 31 Red and yellow silk sachet
The Eastern Han dynasty
Excavated from No. 15 Tomb in Yuli Yingpan,
Xinjiang

Fig. 32   The painting of the two dragons on the lacquer coffin
The Western Han dynasty
Excavated from No.1 Han Tomb in Mawangdui, Changsha City, Hunan

Fig. 33   The image on the lintel of Qianliangtai Tomb
The Eastern Han dynasty
Excavated from Qianliangtai Village, Zhucheng, Shangdong
The image shows the braid knots (top row), diamond-shaped cross binding knots (bottom row left), and double-coin knots (bottom row middle).

The double-coin knots also have a very long history. They are frequently found in the relics of the Spring and Autumn Era, the Western Han dynasty, and the Eastern Han dynasty with different combinations and designs (fig. 33). The image on the capping stone of the West Chamber in the Han Tomb, excavated from Dongjiazhuang, Anqiu City of Shandong, shows the twine of the two dragons which forms a double-coin knot. This verifies the popularity and social importance of the double-coin knots.

Besides the knots that mentioned above, flat knot, overhand knot, cross binding knot, braid knot also appear on the relics of the Han dynasty. Together with the double-coin knot, they had marked the beginning of Chinese knotting with decorative motives.

3. The Developments of Decorative Knotting

Chinese knotting was very popular on clothing and everyday goods in the Six Dynasties (220–581). Buddhism, originated from India, was widespread in this era. The Buddha figures were localized to meet Chinese culture and arts as indicated by the knotting details on their clothes and accessories (fig. 34). The painting of *Ode to the Goddess of the Luo River* by Gu Kaizhi (345–409) also illustrates the influence of knotting. Knots are found on the clothing, umbrella and cart accessories (fig. 35). Sauvastika knot was first introduced in this period as well.

The development of Chinese knotting reached its peak in the Sui (581–681) and Tang (618–907) dynasties. First reason was the creation of new knots, such as left half hitch, sauvastika knot, cross knot, cloverleaf knot, tassel knot, etc. (fig. 36). Second, Chinese knotting was promoted from a supplementary element to a main decorative feature. This is revealed on the jade knotting accessories that are on the belt of the palace maid collected in the Royal Ontario Museum, Toronto, Canada. Third, Chinese knots were not only used as a single piece but also advanced to have more combinations. The knotting patterns shown on the silver-gilt five-legged aroma burner of the Tang dynasty unearthed from the tomb at Famen Temple, Fufeng, Shaanxi, is a good example. Chinese knotting became very popular in the palace (fig. 37). During this period of time, this art was spread to overseas through lots of cultural exchange events, especially Japan and Korea.

In the Liao (916–1125) and Song dynasties (960–1279), the more complicated knots, such as endless knot and prosperity knot, were introduced. On top of that, more modified and

Fig. 34   Guanyin Bodhisattva (gilded and painted stone sculpture)
The Northern Qi–Sui dynasty (550–618)
Qingzhou Museum, Shandong
During the period of 3rd to 9th century, Qingzhou City, Shandong was one of the centers of spreading Buddhism. About a thousand precious stone Buddha figures were unearthed in the late 1980s.

This Guanyin Bodhisattva wears a few magnificent necklaces. The one on the back has a piece of jade attached by a cross binding knot. The two silk sashes form a big decorative knot.

Fig. 35   *Ode to the Goddess of the Luo River* (partial shown)
Color painting on silk
572.8 cm (W) x 27.1 cm (H)
Gu Kaizhi
Palace Museum, Beijing
A number of knotting accessories can be found in this romantic painting: the accessories around the waist of the Goddess of the Luo River, the pendants of the umbrella (like sauvastika knot), and the accessories at the dragon cart (like cloverleaf knot).

Fig. 36   *Paired Cranes with Tassel Knot*
Jade Pendant
Tang dynasty
Private collection
The pair of cranes of this jade pendant hold a tassel knot in their mouths. This kind of tassel knot is commonly found in the Tang dynasty relics, which proves the popularity.

Fig. 37   *The Revelry in the Tang Court* (right)
Painting on paper
Tang dynasty
Unknown artist
Palace Museum, Taipei
This piece of art reflects the daily life of the Tang imperial ladies. They sit around a large square table. Some are tasting tea; some are playing music. All the chairs are decorated with Chinese knot.

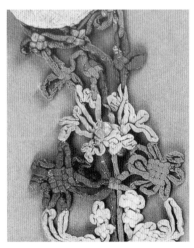

Fig. 38   Gourd-Shaped Sachet Embroidered with Figures and Flowers
Liao dynasty
Excavated in Alashan League, Inner Mongolia
Sachet is a lucky charm that helps receive blessings and exorcise evil spirits. The bottom part of the sachet is made of four-color knots including cloverleaf knot and endless knot.

combination knots were created for different decoration needs (fig. 38).

Although no new basic knots were produced in the Jin (1115–1234) and Yuan (1279–1368) dynasties, the application of knotting was further established. There were not a lot of historical records about knotting in the Ming dynasty (1368–644). However, from the Emperor Hongzhi portrait in the Palace Museum, Beijing, a pair of knotting pendants is found on the screen at the back of the Dragon Throne. This is the evident of the importance of knotting in the royal palace.

4. Becoming an Independent Form of Art

The second boom of Chinese knotting was in the Qing dynasty (1644–1911). The plafond knot first appeared at this time (fig. 39). Most of the basic knots were pushed forward to form different combinations. This is mentioned in *Dream of Red Chamber*, Chapter 35, which talks about double diamond knot, multiple loop knot, and plum blossom knot. Chinese knotting was practiced in a lot of everyday items, such as hats, sedan chairs, draperies, fans, sachets, hair pins, necklaces, and eyeglass cases. The knots not only illuminated these items but also carried the auspicious significance (fig. 40).

In the early Republican Era, the traditional Chinese society and lifestyle were heavily impacted by the western culture. Clothing styles and daily necessities were completely changed. Chinese knotting unfortunately discontinued developing, which led to the verge of disappearing.

Since 1970s, artists of great insight were afraid of the extinction of this beautiful craft and started the rescue crusade. They published art books, organized classes, and invented new basic knots, like creeper knot and constellation knot, to revive this traditional art. Their hard work got paid off. More and more people had shown interest and led to the upsurge in learning Chinese knotting. New knotting combinations and big decorative knots were generated. Specialized materials and accessories started to grow. This urged the establishment of knotting in the commercial market.

Nowadays, Chinese knotting can be found everywhere to make our life more exciting. This classic art has sparkled even more.

Fig. 39　Copper Lion
Qing dynasty
The East Gate of the Summer Palace, Beijing
Plafond knot is a very common element on lion sculptures in the Qing dynasty.

Fig. 40　*A Hundred Birds Worshipping the Phoenix* Eyeglass Case
Qing dynasty
Palace Museum, Beijing
This is an imperial accessory for the Qing emperor. The top is decorated with a pineapple knot.

Fig. 41   Cords are the most significant component for making Chinese knots. Different colors and materials produce different effects.

CHAPTER THREE
GETTING READY

This chapter introduces what you need to prepare before creating the knots. Choosing the appropriate materials and tools is like icing on the cake, making your design a lot more attractive and efficient. We also present the basic and important techniques, such as designing, interlacing, tightening, shaping, and adjusting, as well as some little tricks, which are the essential ingredients of the design and knotting process.

1. Tools

The most important components of making Chinese knots are your skillful hands. However, to create a more complicated knot combining with other elements, proper tools become the essentials. Below are the most popular tools (fig. 42):

Mats & pins: They are good partners to set the cords in place. You can choose cork mats, PVC mats or foam mats, and wrap them with a piece of fabric. Then use pins for securing the cords to avoid shifting them away from the original settings.

Lighter: It is used to melt the cord ends.

Big-eye needles: These needles are thicker and longer than the regular needles, commonly used for pulling cords into the knot.

Needles and threads: Some knots are comparatively loose. You can use needles and threads to secure them with blind stitches. Try to choose threads that are the same color as the cords.

Tweezers: When making complicated knots or shaping, it is easier to use tweezers to pull the cords.

Tape measure: You will need one to measure the cord length.

Scissors: They are must-have for cutting the cords. Be sure they are sharp enough to get a clean cut.

Double-sided tape: It is used for coiling thread, refer to "Other Basic Techniques."

Flat-nose pliers: When dealing with thicker cords, you can use the flat-nose pliers for pulling, shaping, and securing instead of using the little tweezers. You can also use them for fastening the ribbon clamps and jump rings.

Round-nose pliers: These are used to bend head pins and wires.

Wire cutters: These are the best for cutting wires.

Superglue: You can use it to seal the cord ends or attach the cord ends to cord end caps or other metal findings.

PVC mat

Cork mat

Foam mat (wrapped with a piece of cloth)

Pins

Big-eye needle

Needles & threads

Tweezers

Tape measure

Decorative tapes

Double-sided tape

Flat-nose pliers

Round-nose pliers

Wire cutters

Superglue

Lighter

Scissors

Glue gun & glue sticks

Fig. 42   Tools

Glue gun & glue sticks: These are good for sealing the cord ends and attaching metal findings, e.g. bar pins and barrettes.

Decorative tapes: You can use them to decorate the knots.

2. Materials

The main materials for Chinese knotting are the cords. Different cords have different characteristics and purposes. Select the material and color wisely with the consideration of the knot implications, appropriate findings and accessories.

Cords

In the market nowadays, there is a great variety of cords. Besides the most popular nylon cords, you can also choose waxed cords, silk cords or leather cords to provide a different effect. The thickness of the cord is also a key point. The thicker the cord you choose, the bigger the knot you get. Of course, this depends on your design and may require a longer cord. In chapters 4 and 5, the projects presented are mostly 2.5 mm in diameter or width, which is one of the factors to determine the length. You may find the suggested length a bit longer after tightening the knot but it is necessary for adjustment. Below is a list of cords in the mainstream (fig. 43):

Nylon cord: This cord is good for all types of Chinese knotting. It has a shiny surface, twill texture, and a wide range of colors, including multi-colors. The nylon cord is made of synthetic fiber; thus it can be sealed with a flame.

Braided rattail cord: This cord is sturdier than the nylon cord. It comes with the options of matte and shiny finish. However, the color selections are less. The braided rattail cord is aesthetic with a defined texture, most suitable for high quality knotting. The material is synthetic fiber that can be sealed by flame. The typical types are thick and extra-thick, ranging from 1 to 4 mm. The fine ones are jewelry beading strings, ranging from 0.4 to 0.8 mm, that are soft and sturdy, mainly used for beading.

Flat cord: This cord is also known as *ruyi* cord. If you prefer a defined style, choose this to create your knot, especially for clothing decoration. The flat cord is made of synthetic fiber, which can be

Types of Nylon Cords
The most common types are 1 to 7. For beginners, types 4 and 5 are recommended.

Type	Diameter (mm)
1	11
2	6
3	4
4	3
5	2.5
6	2
7	1.5

Nylon cords

Flat cords

Waxed cotton cords

Braided rattail cords (medium)

Braided rattail cords (fine)

Waxed synthetic fiber cords

Braided silk cords

Metallic cords

Leather cords

Fig. 43   Cords

sealed with a flame.

Waxed cord: This kind of cord is processed by dyeing its surface and then finished with a layer of wax on top. There are two types. One is the waxed cotton cord, which is soft with a natural and matte finish. You can only use glue to conceal the ends. The other type is made by synthetic fiber with a shiny finish, commonly used for high-end knot making. The ends can be sealed with a flame.

Leather cord: This cord is made of animal hides with limited color selections, often used for clothing decorations and high-end products.

Metallic cord: Due to the high decorative nature, metallic cord is a good enhancement agent.

Braided silk cord: As stated by the name, this cord is produced by interweaving the silk threads, ranging from 3 to 15 counts. With the wide color selections and soft texture, it is often used for decorations.

Findings

Alternating a decorative Chinese knot to a practical item, such as earring, brooch, and bracelet, findings take a critical part.

Below are the most popular findings (fig. 45):

Clasps: These are for connecting the cord ends of necklaces and bracelets.

Lobster clasps: The application is similar to other clasps but often paired up with a jump ring or chain for easy adjustment.

Jump rings: These are for fastening findings and accessories to a knot.

Safety pins: Attach them to the back of the knots to make brooches.

Bar pins: The application is similar to safety pins but glue is required.

Barrettes: To make a hair accessory, simply adhere a basic barrette to a knot.

Earring hooks: These are the essential components for earring making.

Ribbon clamps: These are designed to fasten cord end or a series of cord ends.

Cord end caps: The function of the cap is to enclose the cord by tucking the end inside the tube.

Head pins & floral bead caps: This is a good combination for linking the knots or decorating the beads.

Metal rings: The metal ring can be used as a core, having the cords twined around it. There are different shape available for creative design.

Cellphone straps: These are used to string up knots, often applied to decorative charms.

Extension chain: Fasten the lobster clasp onto different part of the extension chain to obtain the desired length for the bracelet or necklace.

Accessories

The accessories play an important role of enhancing knotting elements, bring a simple knot up to another level (fig. 46). Choosing a proper accessory can promote your design, whether it is stylish, classic, neat or exquisite, as long as it is well incorporated with the selected cords, knots and findings.

Let's pick jade as an example. Jade is a significant treasure in Chinese culture, representing dignity. It is smooth and translucent, commonly combined with refined knots to fabricate bracelets and necklaces.

Fig. 44 The endless knot has a very long history and lots of variations, commonly combined with other knots to create new types of knots.

Clasps

Lobster clasps

Earring hooks

Jump rings

Bar pins

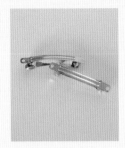

Barrettes

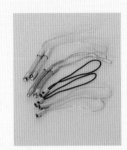

Cellphone straps

Ribbon clamps

Cord end caps

Head pins

Safety pins

Extension chains

Floral bead caps

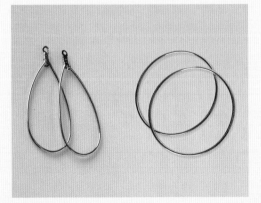

Metal earrings and bracelets

Fig. 45   Findings

Accessories

Tassels

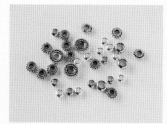

Spacer beads

Metal beads

Porcelain beads

Porcelain charms

Porcelain tube beads

Ancient Chinese coins

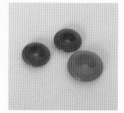

Jade discs

Jade beads

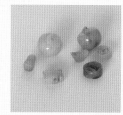

Jade charms

Glass beads

Crystal beads & charms

White copper with inset stone beads

Cloisonné beads & charms

Metal pendants & charms

Fig. 46   Accessories

3. Basic Techniques

Designing & interlacing, tightening & shaping, and adjusting & decorating are the three basic techniques of Chinese knotting. Below are the principles and you can practice more when going through the instructions of each knot.

Designing & Interlacing

This is the first step of knot making, starting from designing, weaving to finishing the knot base.

Before the actual fabrication, you will need to think about the end product, implication, and name. Then choose the appropriate cords, findings, and accessories to construct the knot as a whole.

When interlacing, you will have to set the path clearly and weave slowly in one go. Secure the cords with pins when dealing with complicated process. Try to keep them neat and reserve enough space for the cords to pass through. Use tweezers as necessary to tighten and shape the knots.

Tightening & Shaping

This is the process after designing and interlacing for massaging the knot to achieve the desired result. This includes pulling, adjusting, tightening, and securing. Patience and thoroughness are required.

In general, we need to tighten the knot. When doing so, identify the directions, cord ends, and loops that are to be arranged. Pull the cord from one side through the center of the knot in one direction and adjust the shape while pulling. Try not to stop in the middle to avoid confusion since the cord is most likely to be shifted back and forth. Complicated knots can be assisted with tweezers.

After tightening, we need to align the loops. In this procedure, be sure to keep the center of the knot to its original form with appropriate tightness. Finally, fine tune the knot per the desired style to obtain the best shape.

Adjusting & Decorating

Adjusting and decorating is the final procedure after interlacing and shaping to further secure and decorate the knots.

To help the knots last longer, we need to secure those that are easily distorted. General speaking, there are two methods. First is sewing, using a thread of the same color to blind stitch the knot. The other is gluing, applying a small amount of glue at the intersections. Remember to avoid exposing the stitches and glue to maintain the beauty of the knots. Always conceal the cord ends to present a perfect piece of art.

Don't forget to add findings and accessories to enhance your design.

4. Other Basic Techniques

Below are the basic techniques that you will encounter in the process of making Chinese knots. Sealing the cord ends is commonly applied on nylon cords since they can be easily melted by heat.

Sealing Cord End

Seal the cord end with a flame before interlacing to make the cord end stronger without breaking apart during the weaving process. The other method is to apply a small amount of glue on the end.

Trim the cord end as necessary. Set a small flame with the lighter, slowly move the cord end towards the flame and melt it. Turn off the flame and wait for a few seconds for the end to cool down. The fiber of the first 2 mm of the cord will be sealed off and become glossy and stiff.

Concealing Cord End to the Knot

Conceal the cord end to the knot is the last step of making a knot.

Trim the end 1 to 2 mm away from the knot. Melt it with a flame and push it to the knot using the smooth side of the tweezers. Try to keep the joint as small as possible so that it is more presentable.

Joining Two Cords

This is commonly used when connecting the cords.

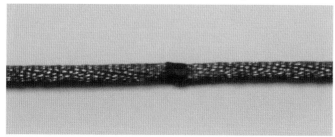

Set the two cord ends together and hold them with tweezers. Melt them with a flame and connect them immediately so that they will stick to each other. After cooling down, the ends will be joined together.

Coiling

This technique is for securing two cords together, using a braided silk cord or a fine thread. It is commonly practiced when concealing a joint or decorating a loop, serving both practical and decorative purposes. There are a lot of cord selections and the most popular ones are the fine ones.

2 Take the braided silk cord over its end and wrap around the nylon cord.

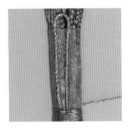

3 Continue to coil along the double-sided tape. Note that the silk cord has to be neatly arranged.

The loop on the top

4 Stop coiling when it reaches the edge of the tape and pull it out from the loop on the top.

1 Set together the two nylon cords. Wrap the double-sided tape around the area to be coiled. Ensure the length of the double-sided tape is the same as that of the coil. As shown in the figure, loop the braided silk cord and place it on the tape. The top of the loop is a bit longer than the tape.

5 Pull the bottom silk cord end to shift the top loop into the coil. Then pull both silk cord ends at the same time.

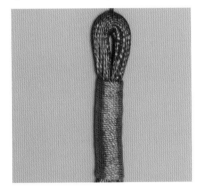

6 Trim the ends. Use the tweezers to conceal any exposed tape and silk cord ends into the coil.

Fig. 47 Left: this six-loop cage knot in blue shades is formed by using supplementary cording. Middle: this pink charm is a combination of good-luck knot, endless knot, and porcelain teapot charm. Right: the body of this pink charm is a modified endless knot, decorated with porcelain beads.

Two-Strand Plait

Two-strand plait is commonly used for making the sides of a necklace.

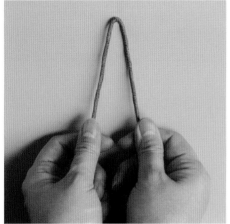   

1 Pin the center of the cord. Hold both ends and twist them to the right.

2 Continue to twist to the desired length. Done!

Applying Tassels

Tassels are usually applied at the last step to perfect the knot.

1 Pin the knot on the mat, leaving approximately 8 cm of cord ends.

2 Hold the cord ends together and pull them out from the center of the tassel head.

Cord ends

3 Form an overhand knot with the cord ends and push it up.

4 Trim the ends and seal them to the knot with a flame.

5 Tidy up the tassel to cover the overhand knot. Done!

Fig. 48   Knotting products in richly colored cords.

CHAPTER FOUR
INTRODUCTORY LESSONS

In this chapter, we will demonstrate the most popular and representative Chinese knots, starting from the fundamental to the advanced ones, using the step-by-step instructions with illustrations.

After going through the steps, we will provide an application for each knot, such as barrette, ring, earring, necklace, coaster, and bookmark. Enjoy your own productions while learning the techniques to embellish your life style.

Meaning of Symbols	**Symbols**	**Meanings**
To help you understand the knotting instructions easier, besides the descriptions below the figures, symbols are used to identify the movements and details.	→	Single arrow: moving direction of single cord.
	⇒	Paired arrows: moving direction of double cords.
	A B	Letter next to cord: identification of cord.
	2	Number or letter next to loop: identification of loop.
	2	White number or letter next to loop or cord: identification of cord in previous location.
		Yellow dot: center of cord.
		Hollow circle or oval: intersection of active cord over other cord.
	⇦	Horizontal arrow with dotted line: flipping horizontally.
	⇩	Vertical arrow with dotted line: flipping vertically.
	↙	Arrow with right angle: turning 90° (the dotted line represents the original cord location).
	■ ■ ■ ■	Sparse dotted line: portion of cord not shown in the figure.
	■■■■■■	Dense dotted line: comparison of cord location (before or after).
	□→	Arrow with rectangle: enlarged figure.

1. Overhand Knot

The overhand knot is a basic supplementary knot. This simple and tiny knot has a wide range of applications, such as connecting different knots, closing the cord ends and being part of some complicated knots. It has two types, the left overhand knot and the right overhand knot.

Knot Type
Basic supplementary knot

Suggested Materials
1 cord: 2.5 mm (Dia.), 20 cm (L)

Right Overhand Knot

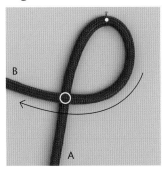

1 Pin the middle of the cord. The left side is A and the right is B. Take cord B to the left over cord A.

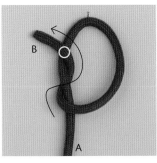

2 Bring cord B up to go under cord A. Pull cord B out from the loop.

3 Pull the ends to tighten the knot. Note that the right loop is on top of the left loop. Done!

Left Overhand Knot

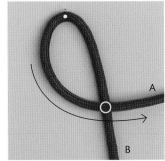

1 Pin the middle of the cord. The left side is A and the right is B. Take cord A to the right over cord B.

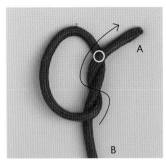

2 Bring cord A up to go under cord B. Pull cord A out from the loop.

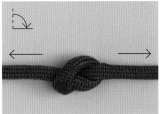

3 Pull the ends to tighten the knot. Note that the left loop is on top of the right loop. Done!

Keychain

Cord: 1 red cord, 2.5 mm (Dia.), 50 cm (L)
Finding: 1 split key ring
Accessories: 2 silver beads

1 Pin the middle of the cord. The left side is A and the right is B. Set them side by side and create a left double overhand knot.

2 Tighten the knot. Insert the 2 silver beads into the ends, one on each side. Close the ends with the overhand knots.

3 Attach the split key ring onto the top loop. The keychain is done.

2. Binding Knot

The binding knot has a very long history with a wide range of applications. It is also known as the lark's head knot, which associates with leaping for joy. There are two ways of making a binding knot and cannot be done by itself. It requires another item to complete. As shown below, the green cord is the anchoring cord and the yellow one is the twining cord. Learn and compare both techniques.

Knot Type
Basic supplementary knot

Suggested Materials
1 active cord: 2.5 mm (Dia.), 30 cm (L)
1 anchoring cord: 2.5 mm (Dia.), 30 cm (L)

Upper Binding Knot

1 Fold the yellow cord in half and place above the green cord.

2 Flip the loop behind the green cord to form a half circle.

3 Pass the ends through the half circle loop. The base is done.

4 Pull the ends to tighten the knot. Finished!

Lower Binding Knot

 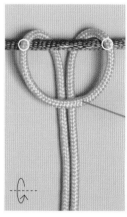

1 Fold the yellow cord in half and place under the green cord.

2 Bring the loop in front of the green cord to form a half circle.

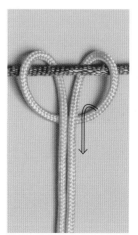 

3 Pull the ends through the half circle loop. The base is done.

4 Pull the ends to tighten the knot. Finished!

Jade Necklace
Cord: 1 yellow cord, 2.5 mm (Dia.)
Accessory: 1 jade disc

Attach the jade disc to the cord using an upper binding knot.

Attach the jade disc to the cord using a lower binding knot.

Fig. 49 These neat decorative charms are composed of basic supplementary knots: binding knot, overhand knot, and cross binding knot.

3. Horizontal Binding Knot

The horizontal binding knot is a popular knot that is used to form a continuous loop, representing perfect and complete. Same as the binding knot, it requires an anchoring piece, for example, a metal bracelet as shown below.

Knot Type
Basic supplementary knot

Suggested Materials
1 cord: 2.5 mm (Dia.), 30 cm (L)
1 metal bracelet

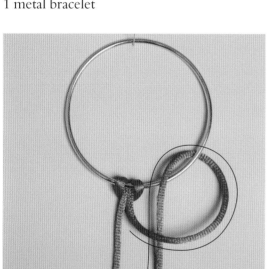
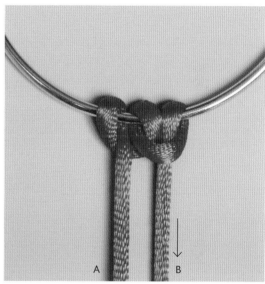

1 Fold the cord in half. The left side is A and the right is B. Place the bracelet over the cord. Create a lower binding knot. Take end B to the upper right and under the bracelet. Pass it around the bracelet and pull under the cord to tighten the knot.

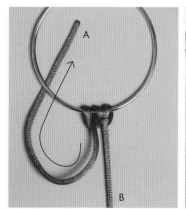
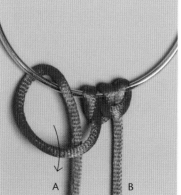
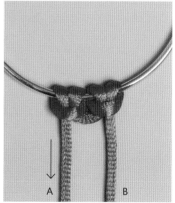

2 Next is to work on cord A. Take end A to the upper left and under the bracelet. Pass it around the bracelet and pull under the cord to tighten the knot. You can find that steps 1 and 2 are similar, where the ends go up, under the bracelet and turn back down.

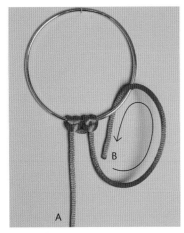

3 Going back to cord B, take it to the upper right, going over the bracelet. Pull it out from the loop and tight over the cord. Now back to cord A. Take it to the upper left, going over the bracelet. Pull it tight over the cord as shown. Done.

Lucky Bracelet

Cord: 1 orange cord, 4 mm (Dia.), 250 cm (L)
Finding: 1 metal bracelet

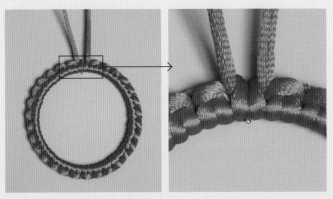

1 Choose a proper size bracelet. Create horizontal binding knots continiously. The whole bracelet is now covered. Note that both ends are stretched upwards.

2 Turn the left end to the right and tuck into the knot.

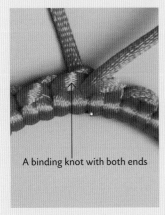

A binding knot with both ends

3 Tighten it to form a binding knot with both ends.

4 Trim the ends. Seal with a flame. Turn the joint until it conceals under the knot. The lucky bracelet is complete!

4. Cross Binding Knot

The cross binding knot is one of the oldest basic supplementary knots. Because of its implication of luck and wise, it was commonly used to string up pierced jades as pendants in the old days.

This knot is very simple and has both practical and decorative functions but requires a pierced item to complete. Below, we will demonstrate the cross binding knot with a piece of jade.

Knot Type
Basic supplementary knot

Suggested Materials
2 cords: 2.5 mm (Dia.), 10 cm (L)
1 piece of jade disc

1 Place the 2 cords parallel on the board. Place the jade disc on the left cord. Pull the cord out from the opening in the middle to form a loop.

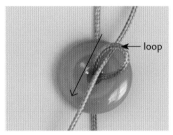

2 Insert the right cord diagonally into the loop. The base is set.

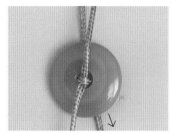

3 Next is shaping. Pull the ends of the left cord to tighten the loop. The 2 cords are on different sides of the jade. Done!

Cellphone Charm
Cords: 1 yellow cord, 2 mm (Dia.), 90 cm (L); 1 green cord, 1 mm (Dia.), 80 cm (L)
Finding: 1 gold cellphone strap with a jump ring
Accessories: 1 jade disc, 4 gold metal beads

1 Create a button knot and attach the jade disc below using the cross binding knot. Make another button knot below the jade disc to keep it in place.

2 Then make a seven-loop good-luck knot and a double-connection knot further down below.

3 Insert 1 gold metal bead, 1 green pineapple knot, and another gold metal bead into one end. Close it with a multiple overhand knot. Do the same for the other end.

4 Pass the yellow cord through the jump ring of the cellphone strap. This is the finished cellphone charm.

5. Left Half Hitch

Both the left half hitch and the right half hitch, which will be introduced on the next page, are basic supplementary knots. They require an anchoring cord to complete. The techniques of these 2 knots are simple and similar. The only difference is the orientation. The knots are tiny and good for making bracelets and necklaces, as well as supporting other decorative elements. To have a clearer demonstration, 2 different colors are selected here.

Knot Type
Basic supplementary knot

Suggested Materials
1 active cord: 2.5 mm (Dia.), 20 cm (L)
1 anchoring cord: 2.5 mm (Dia.), 20 cm (L)

 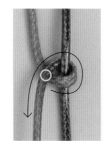   

1 The blue cord on the left is the active cord and the purple cord on the right is the anchoring cord. Place both of them vertically on the board. Move the blue cord to the right over the purple cord.

2 Wrap the blue cord anticlockwise around the purple cord and let the blue cord hang down to form a blue loop. One left half hitch is done.

3 Repeat the above step to form another blue loop by wrapping the blue cord anticlockwise around the purple cord.

4 Continue to twine using the same method. Push the knots upwards periodically. A series of left half hitches are formed. As shown in the figure, the binding is on the left.

5 A proper adjustment can create a different result. After making each half hitch, push it upwards and tighten the ends. This creates the twisting effect as shown in the figure.

Cellphone Charm

Cords: 1 purple cord, 2.5 mm (Dia.), 20 cm (L); 1 blue cord, 2.5 mm (Dia.), 40 cm (L)

Finding: 1 cellphone strap

Accessory: 1 small bell

1 First is to make a series of left half hitches. Then curve it to form a circle.

2 Trim the purple ends and seal them together with a flame. Trim the blue ends, reserving part of the ends for cord end cap.

3 Secure the blue cord ends to the cord end cap and attach the small bell onto the bottom of the loop. Connect the cord end cap to the cell phone strap attachment. The cellphone charm is finished.

6. Right Half Hitch

Base on the technique of the left half hitch, switch the orientation to produce the right half hitch. Simply place the active cord on the right to twine, the binding will be shifted to the right. To have a clearer demonstration, 2 differernt colors are selected here.

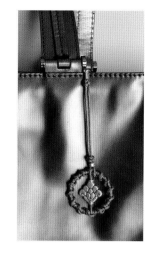

Knot Type
Basic supplementary knot

Suggested Materials
1 active cord: 2.5 mm (Dia.), 20 cm (L)
1 anchoring cord: 2.5 mm (Dia.), 20 cm (L)

1 The blue cord on the left is the anchoring cord and the purple cord on the right is the active cord. Place both of them vertically on the board. Take the purple cord to the left over the blue cord.

2 Wrap the purple cord clockwise around the blue cord and let the purple cord hang down to form a purple loop. One right half hitch is done.

3 Repeat the above step to form another purple loop by wrapping the purple cord clockwise around the blue cord.

4 Continue to twine by repeating the same step. Push the knots upwards periodically. A series of right half hitches are formed. As shown in the figure, the binding is on the right.

5 A proper adjustment can create a different result. After making each half hitch, push it upwards and tighten the ends. This creates the twisting effect as shown in the figure.

Pendant
Cord: 1 purple cord, 2 mm (Dia.), 150 cm (L)
Findings: 1 metal ring, 1 lobster clasp
Accessories: 1 silver lotus bead, 1 silver bead

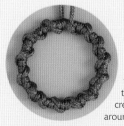

1 Create the right half hitches around the metal ring. Push and tighten every hitch to create the twisting effect around the ring.

2 Take one cord end downwards, going through the silver lotus bead and one of the hitches at the bottom. Then bring it back upwards, going through the silver lotus bead again and one of the hitches on top. Pass both ends through the silver bead and form a button knot above.

3 Trim the ends to the desired length. Tie a button knot at the end and attach the lobster clasp to it.

7. Alternate Half Hitch

The alternate half hitch is a combination of the left and right half hitches. By rotating the anchoring and active cords, tying half hitches on both sides, create neat and tiny knots that can be applied for bracelets and necklaces.

The cords can be the same or different colors. For easy reference, blue and purple cords are selected for the instructions below.

Knot Type
Traditional modified combination knot

Suggested Materials
2 cords: 2.5 mm (Dia.), 60 cm (L)

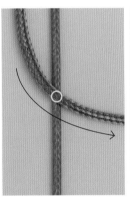 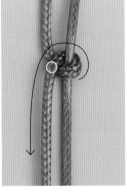  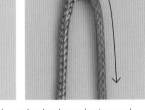

1 Place vertically the purple cord on the left side and blue cord on the right. Set with pins. First is to make a left half hitch with the purple cord, having the blue cord as the anchoring cord.

2 Then change the purple cord to be the anchoring cord, create a right half hitch with the blue cord.

  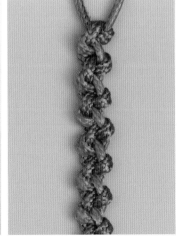

3 Alternately make left and right half hitches by rotating the blue and purple cords to be the anchoring cord. A series of alternate half hitches is done. Create a series of alternate half hitch until it reached the desired length. Attach the cord end caps with the extension chain and the lobster clasp to the ends. The bracelet is done.

8. Multiple Overhand Knot

Making a multiple overhand knot is very simple. All you need is one cord. The knot is compact and tight. It is often used to tie the ends of pendants, bracelets, and necklaces. It has an implication of peace and luck. In Buddhism and Taoism, a lot of knotting ornaments are composed of multiple overhand knots that are arranged in the multiples of 7 as a symbol of protection.

Knot Type
Basic supplementary knot

Suggested Materials
1 cord: 2.5 mm (Dia.), 20 cm (L)

1 Place the cord straight. The multiple overhand knot is shaped at the end of the cord. Curve the end anticlockwise to the left and pull out from the loop.

2 Bring the end upwards and under the loop.

3 Pass the end over the loop. The base is done.

4 Tighten the knot by pulling both ends gently. The knot is complete. The pattern on one side is 2 loops and the other is an X.

Porcelain Bead Ring
Cord: 1 pink cord, 2.5 mm (Dia.), 30 cm (L)
Accessory: 1 porcelain bead
Tools: double-sided tape, 1 braided silk cord

1 First is to make a multiple overhand knot. Then insert a pierced porcelain bead. Make another multiple overhand knot to position the bead. Once the desired ring size is determined, trim the ends. Seal the ends with a flame.

2 Put double-sided tape around the joint.

3 Coil a thread around the double-sided tape and secure it with a flame. The ring is done!

9. Figure-Eight Knot

The figure-eight knot is a popular basic supplementary knot. The name is simply come from the shape, which looks like the Arabic number 8. In Chinese, eight (*ba*, 八) sounds like rich (*fa*, 发), which is believed to bring luck and wealth. The figure-eight knot is usually shaped at the end of a cord. It is small and tight, and commonly applied on decorative elements, as well as buttons, bracelets, necklaces, etc.

Knot Type
Basic supplementary knot

Suggested Materials
1 cord: 2.5 mm (Dia.), 30 cm (L)

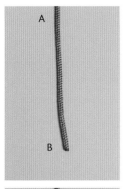

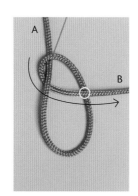

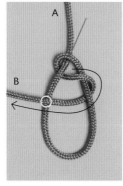

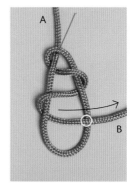

1 Place the cord vertically. The top part is A and the bottom is B. Turn cord B upwards and anticlockwise to form a loop. Set with a pin.

2 Pull cord B to the right, going under and over the loop. Then turn it down and back to the left, going under and over the loop.

3 Repeat step 2. Take the cord from one side to another, forming at least 3 loop s on each side. This is the base. The number of the loops is set according to your design.

4 Next is shaping. First is to tighten the horizontal loops from top to bottom. Then pull cord A upward until it is tight. Trim cord B and seal with a flame. Flip around the knot. This is the finish product of the figure-eight knot.

Earring

Cord: 1 yellow cord, 2.5 mm (Dia.), 50 cm (L)
Finding: 1 earing hook
Tools: double-sided tape, 1 braided silk cord

1 First is to make a figure-eight knot.

2 Pass cord A through the hole of the earring hook. Make another figure-eight knot on the other end. Position the earring hook in the middle.

3 As shown in the figure, use double-sided tape to bind the cords together.

4 Coil the thread around the tape and secure with a flame. The earring is done!

Earring

Cord: 1 red cord, 2 mm (Dia.), 60 cm (L)
Finding: 1 earring hook
Accessories: 4 spacer beads

1 Attach the earring hook to the cord and set it in the middle. Make a double-connection knot and thread 2 spacer beads on the cord.

2 Then thread the 2 spacer beads on the cord ends and create 2 figure-eight knots, one at each side. Adjust the knots and shift the spacer beads to the bottom. The earring is done. Note that the spacer beads below the figure-eight knots are for decorating, whereas the ones below the double connection knot are for positioning.

10. Single Figure-Eight Knot

The single figure-eight knot is a basic supplementary knot. It is named due to its shape. The knot is small and flexible, and commonly used for tying the ends of ornaments, bracelets, and necklaces.

Knot Type
Basic supplementary knot

Suggested Materials
1 cord: 2.5 mm (Dia.), 20 cm (L)

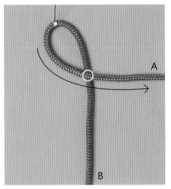

1 Pin the cord in the middle. The left side is A and the right is B. Move cord A to the right over cord B.

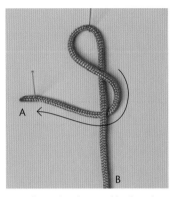

2 Take cord A down and back to the left, passing under cord B.

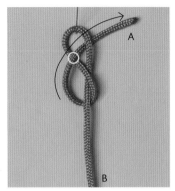

3 Bend cord A to the upper right, going over and under the loop above. The base is done.

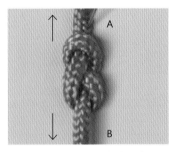

4 Next is shaping. Pull both ends at the same time until it is tight.

5 Trim one end and seal with a flame. The knot is finished!

Decorative Accessory
Cord: 1 yellow cord, 2.5 mm (Dia.), 30 cm (L)

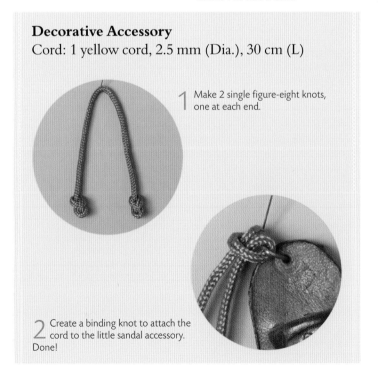

1 Make 2 single figure-eight knots, one at each end.

2 Create a binding knot to attach the cord to the little sandal accessory. Done!

11. Braid Knot

A series of braid knots looks like a fully grown ear of rice, which implies a plentiful harvest. The braid knot is arranged by one cord in a narrow and neat form, commonly used to decorate complicated ornaments.

Knot Type
Basic supplementary knot

Suggested Materials
1 cord: 2.5 mm (Dia.), 20 cm (L)

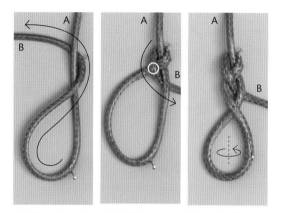

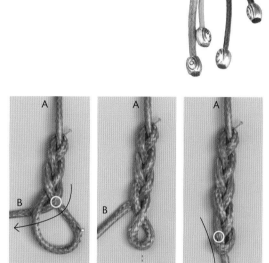

1 Place the cord vertically. The top part is A and the bottom is B. Turn cord B to the left and clockwise over cord A to form a loop. Bend cord B to the left under cord A and pass it through the loop from the front. Flip the loop to the right and it becomes smaller.

2 Take cord B to the lower left, passing it through the loop from the front. Flip the loop to the left and it becomes even smaller. Take cord B to the lower right, passing it through the loop from the front. Done! The idea is to flip the loop to the side of cord B and pass cord B through the loop. Thus, the length of the braid knot is the same as that of the loop.

Cellphone Charm
Cords: 4 cords of different colors, 2.5 mm (Dia.), 20 cm (L)
Findings: 1 cellphone strap, 1 jump ring, 1 cord end cap
Accessories: 4 small beads

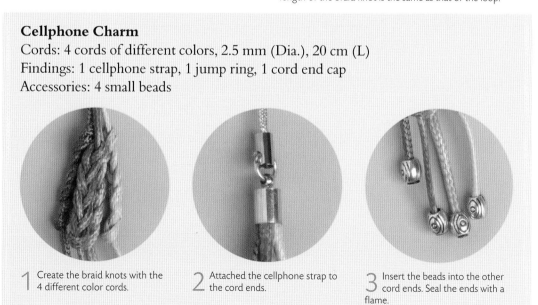

1 Create the braid knots with the 4 different color cords.

2 Attached the cellphone strap to the cord ends.

3 Insert the beads into the other cord ends. Seal the ends with a flame.

12. Four-Strand Plait

As the name suggests, the four-strand plait is made of four twisted cords. It has a wide range of applications, such as bracelets, necklaces, and tying the ends of the combination knots. The cords can be the same or different colors according to your design. Here, we have pink, blue, yellow, and purple cords for clear reference.

Knot Type
Basic supplementary knot

Suggested Materials
4 cords: 2.5 mm (Dia.), 40 cm (L)

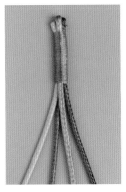

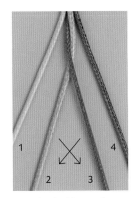

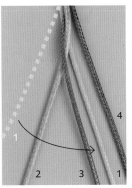

1 Coil the cord ends with a braided silk cord to fasten the 4 cords together. Arrange them as shown in the figure.

2 Take the blue cord to the right over the yellow cord. Let's number the cords 1 to 4 starting from the left.

3 Shift the pink cord 1 to the right between the blue cord 3 and the purple cord 4 from behind. Then turn it to the left over the blue cord 3. This is "cord 1 over cord 3."

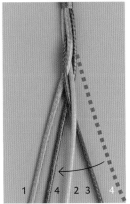

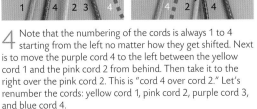

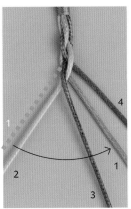

4 Note that the numbering of the cords is always 1 to 4 starting from the left no matter how they get shifted. Next is to move the purple cord 4 to the left between the yellow cord 1 and the pink cord 2 from behind. Then take it to the right over the pink cord 2. This is "cord 4 over cord 2." Let's renumber the cords: yellow cord 1, pink cord 2, purple cord 3, and blue cord 4.

5 Repeat the step "cord 1 over cord 3," i.e., moving the yellow cord 1 to the right between the purple cord 3 and the blue cord 4 from behind, and turning it to the left over the purple cord 3.

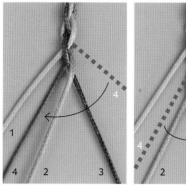

6 Let's renumber the cords again: pink cord 1, yellow cord 2, purple cord 3, and blue cord 4. Repeat the step "cord 4 over cord 2," i.e., taking the blue cord 4 to the left between the pink cord 1 and the yellow cord 2 from behind, and turning it to the right over the yellow cord 2.

7 Renumber the cords and repeat the step "cord 1 over cord 3," i.e., taking the pink cord 1 to the right between the blue cord and the purple cord 4 from behind, and turning it to the left over the blue cord 3.

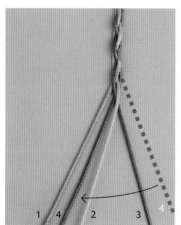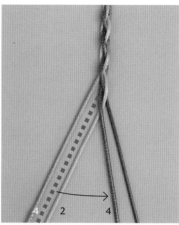

8 Renumber the cords and repeat the step "cord 4 over cord 2," i.e., taking the purple cord 4 to the right between the yellow cord 1 and the pink cord 2 from behind, and turning it to the right over the pink cord 2. Continue by alternating the steps "cord 1 over cord 3" and "cord 4 over cord 2." The four-strand plait is done. Note that the outer cords (cord 1 & cord 4) are always over the others. They are the active cords. If cord 1 is on top of the braid, use "cord 1 over cord 3." If cord 4 is on top of the braid, use "cord 4 over cord 2."

Multi-Color Bracelet

Cords: 4 cords of different colors, 2.5 mm (Dia.), 40 cm (L)
Findings: 2 cord end caps, 1 lobster clasp, 1 extension chain
Tool: 1 braided silk cord

1 Create a four-strand plait to the desired length. Coil the ends with a braided silk cord.

2 Attach the cord end caps to the cord ends, one with the lobster clasp and the other with the extension chain. Done!

13. Clove Hitch

The clove hitch is a supplementary knot. It requires 2 consecutive knots to form the pattern, which carries the auspicious implications of "double happiness" and "good things come in pairs."

To make a clove hitch, an anchoring cord is needed. It has 2 types, the left-hand and right-hand, depending on the arrangement. The technique is not complicated and can be combined differently to make bracelets, belts and ornaments.

Knot Type
Basic supplementary knot

Suggested Materials
1 active cord: 2.5 mm (Dia.), 30 cm (L)
1 anchoring cord: 2.5 mm (Dia.), 10 cm (L)

Left-Hand Clove Hitch

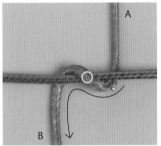

1 Place vertically the blue cord, which is the active cord. Lay horizontally the purple cord, which is the anchoring cord, over the blue cord. Move cord B (the bottom part of the blue cord) to the upper left and wrap around the purple cord.

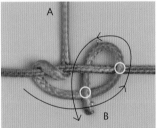

2 As shown, bend cord B to the right, forming an arc over the purple cord. Turn cord B anticlockwise, going under the purple cord and over the blue cord.

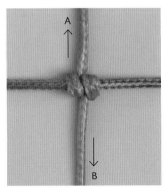

3 Pull both ends to tighten the knot. (on the right)

Right-Hand Clove Hitch

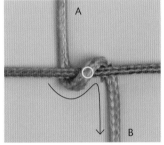

1 Place vertically the blue cord, which is the active cord. Lay horizontally the purple cord, which is the anchoring cord, over the blue cord. Move cord B (the bottom part of the blue cord) to the upper right and wrap around the purple cord.

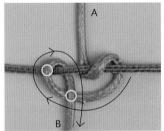

2 As shown, bend cord B to the left, forming an arc over the purple cord. Turn cord B clockwise, going under the purple cord and over the blue cord.

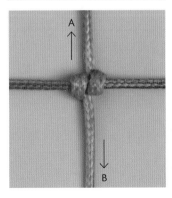

3 Pull both ends to tighten the knot. The left-hand clove hitch (on the left) is a little bit different from the right-hand clove hitch (on the right).

Bracelet
Cords: 6 blue cords, 2.5 mm (Dia.), 60 cm (L)
Findings: 1 pair of metal ribbon clamps with a lobster clasp and an extension chain

1 Line up 6 cords. Secure the ends with a flame. Apply glue as needed for extra support. For easy reference, let's name the cords A to F starting from the left.

2 Apply the ribbon clamp to the ends. Shift cord A to the lower right over the other cords.

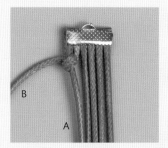

3 Having cord A as the anchoring cord and cord B as the active cord, make a left-hand clove hitch.

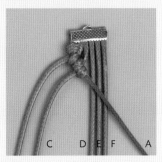

4 Create another left-hand clove hitch with cord A as the anchoring cord and cord C as the active cord. Continue to make more left-hand clove hitches using the same technique with cords D, E & F.

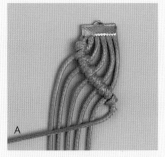

5 Now cord A is at the very right. Turn it to the lower left over the other cords.

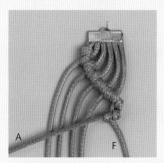

6 Having cord A as the anchoring cord and cord F as the active cord, make a right-hand clove hitch.

7 Continue to make more right-hand clove hitches using the same technique with other active cords starting from the right.

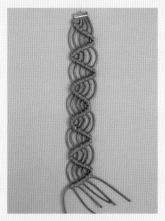

8 Keep making the left-hand and right-hand clove hitches alternatively until it reaches the desired length. Trim the ends and seal them with a flame. Apply glues as necessary for extra support.

9 Attach the other clamp onto the ends. Apply the lobster clasp on one side and the chain on the other side. The clove hitch bracelet is done!

14 . Dew Knot

The dew knot is one of the traditional basic supplementary knots. The harder you pull the ends, the tighter the knot you get. This firm knot is commonly used to end complicated knot ornaments.

Knot Type
Basic supplementary knot

Suggested Materials
1 cord: 2.5 mm (Dia.), 30 cm (L)

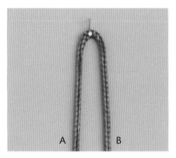

1 Pin the middle of the cord. The left side is A and the right is B.

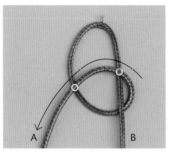

2 Take cord A to the right under cord B, looping anticlockwise over the cord. Let it hang down on the left.

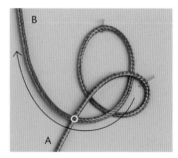

3 Move cord B to the upper left over end A.

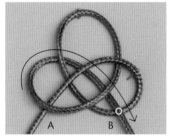

4 Bend cord B clockwise to the lower right, going under-under-under-over the loops as shown in the figure.

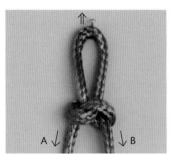

5 Pull the top loop and the ends to tighten the knot. Done!

Cellphone Charm
Cord: 1 purple cord, 2.5 mm (Dia.), 30 cm (L)
Finding: 1 cellphone strap with 1 cord end cap
Accessory: 1 silver bell

1 Thread the silver bell on the cord and create a dew knot.

2 Attach the cellphone strap to the ends. The cellphone charm is done.

15. Snake Knot

The snake knot is formed by a series of dew knots and usually applied on necklace and belt making.

Knot Type
Modified single knot

Suggested Materials
1 cord: 2.5 mm (Dia.), 40 cm (L)

1 First is to make a dew knot and let the cord ends hang down. The left side is cord A and the right is cord B. Move cord A to the right under cord B. Wrap it anticlockwise over cord B and the upper part of cord A. Let it hang down on the left.

2 Take cord B to the upper left over end A and turn it clockwise, going under-under-under-over the loops.

3 Pull both the top loop and the ends to tighten the knot.

4 Repeat the same steps to produce more dew knots to form the snake knot.

Bracelet
Cord: 1 purple cord,
    2.5 mm (Dia.), 160 cm (L)
Accessory: 1 porcelain tube
    bead

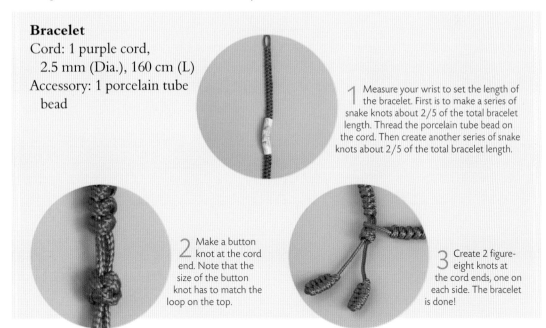

1 Measure your wrist to set the length of the bracelet. First is to make a series of snake knots about 2/5 of the total bracelet length. Thread the porcelain tube bead on the cord. Then create another series of snake knots about 2/5 of the total bracelet length.

2 Make a button knot at the cord end. Note that the size of the button knot has to match the loop on the top.

3 Create 2 figure-eight knots at the cord ends, one on each side. The bracelet is done!

16. *Jingang* Knot

The *jingang* knot looks very similar to the snake knot and it is more secured than the snake knot. In Buddhism, the *jingang* knot is an amulet. It can be formed with 1 cord or 2 connected cords.

Knot Type
Modified single knot

Suggested Materials
1 cord: 2.5 mm (Dia.), 120 cm (L) or
2 cords: 2.5 mm (Dia.), 60 cm (L)

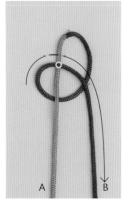

1 The yellow cord is A and the green cord is B. Move cord B to the left under cord A, going clockwise over both cords to form a green loop.

2 Continue to turn cord B clockwise along the internal side of the green loop. Let end B hang down to the lower right.

3 Move cord A to the right over cord B, going anticlockwise under the green loops. Pull it out from the left side of cord A from the front.

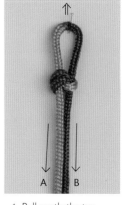

4 Pull gently the top loop and both ends to tighten the knot as shown. Cord A is on the left and cord B is on the right.

5 Flip over the knot. Now cord B is on the left and cord A is on the right. There are 2 green loops around cord A.

6 Enlarge the lower green loop by pulling it outwards. Take cord A to the left under cord B. Turn it clockwise and pass it through the enlarged green loop from the top.

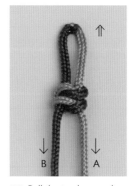

7 Pull the top loop and the ends to tighten the knot. As shown, the green cord B is on the left and the yellow cord A is on the right.

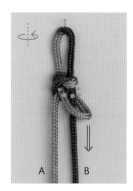

8 Flip over the knot again. Cord A is on the left and cord B is on the right with 2 yellow loops. Enlarge the lower yellow loop by pulling it outwards.

9 Take cord B to the left under cord A. Turn it clockwise over the knot and pass it through the enlarged yellow loop from the top. Pull the top loop and the ends to tighten the knot. As shown, cord A is on the left and cord B is on the right.

10 Continue to enlarge the lower loop on the right and pass the cord on the left through the enlarged loop from the top. Then flip over the knot. Repeat these steps for 7 times.

Comparison

Jingang knot

Snake knot

By looking at the profile, the *jingang* knot has 2 loops at both ends, whereas the snake knot has only 1 loop. Structure-wise, the *jingang* knot is sturdier and tighter than the snake knot when arranged in a series.

Bracelet

Cords: 1 yellow cord, 2.5 mm (Dia.), 90 cm (L); 1 green cord, 2.5 mm (Dia.), 60 cm (L)

Findings: 1 cord end cap with a lobster clasp, 1 cord end cap with an extension chain

Accessories: 2 big silver spacer beads, 3 green beads, 6 small spacer beads

1 This bracelet is formed by 4 equal series of Jinggang knots with 3 identical decorative bead sets. First, measure your wrist to determine the length of the bracelet. Then set the length of each series of Jinggang knots with the consideration of the size of each decorative bead set. Start making the bracelet by creating a series of Jinggang knots. Then add the bead set—2 small spacer beads with the green bead in the middle. Continue to make more series of Jinggang knots with bead sets as shown.

2 Thread the big silver spacer bead on one end and attach the cord end cap with a lobster clasp to enclose the cord ends.

3 Thread another big silver spacer bead on the other end and attach the cord end cap with an extension chain of suitable length to enclose the other cord ends. Done.

17. Sliding Knot

The sliding knot consists of two overhand knots holding the cord against one another. It is a basic supplementary knot with the sliding function that can adjust the length of the cord or loop by pulling the overhand knots apart or together. Thus, it is commonly used in making necklaces and bracelets. Since the two overhand knots are set on the same cord relying on each other, the sliding knot connotes the perfect bond of unity and love.

Knot Type
Basic supplementary knot

Suggested Materials
1 cord: 2.5 mm (Dia.), 30 cm (L)

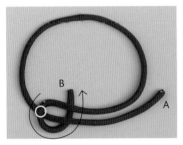 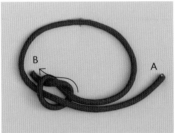 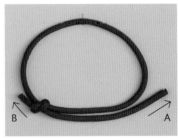

1 Pin the middle of the cord. The left side is A and the right side is B. Loop the cord to form a circle, having the ends partially overlapped as shown. Take cord B down and over cord A. Wrap it around cord A and go under the upper part of cord B. Create an overhand knot with cord B around cord A. Tighten the knot.

2 Let's work on cord A. Bring cord A up and under cord B. Wrap it over cord B and the upper part of cord A. Then create an overhand knot around cord B. Tighten the knot. The base is set. You can pull both ends to slide the 2 overhand knots in the middle.

Bracelet
Cord: 1 red cord, 2.5 mm (Dia.), 50 cm (L)
Accessory: 1 bead

1 Insert the bead into the cord and set it in the middle. Create 2 multiple overhand knots, one on each side (left figure).

2 Create the sliding knot and trim the ends to the desire length. The bracelet is done (right figure).

18. Flat Knot

The flat knot is a type of old basic knot. In the old days, people used it as part of fashion. Besides the practical application, it is also associated with peace, prosperity and luck. In addition to the basic configuration, it can be integrated with other supplementary cords and arranged in a series to provide more variations, such as extended flat knot, twisted flat knot, and extended flat knot with outer loops, that will be introduced later.

Knot Type
Basic single knot

Suggested Materials
1 cord: 2.5 mm (Dia.), 30 cm (L)

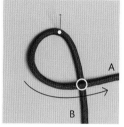

1 Pin the cord in the middle. The left side is A and the right is B. Take cord A to the right over cord B to form a loop.

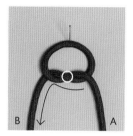

2 Take cord B to the left and pass it through the loop from the front as shown.

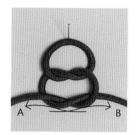

3 Move cord A on the right side to the left over cord B to form another loop. Take cord B to the right and pass it through the loop from the front as shown. The base is set.

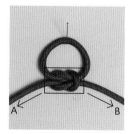

4 Pull both ends to tighten the 2nd loop. The part in the box is the flat knot. The 1st loop on top is supplementary.

Peace Ring
Cord: 1 brownish red cord, 2.5 mm (Dia.), 30 cm (L)
Tools: double-sided tape, 1 braided silk cord

1 Adjust the loop on top to the desired ring size. Then trim the ends also to the desired ring size. Seal the ends with a flame.

2 Flip the top loop down and set parallel to the loop below. Place a piece of double-sided tape around both loops as shown.

3 Coil a braided silk cord around the double-sided tape and secure with a flame. This is the peace ring.

19. Extended Flat Knot

The extended flat knot is modified from the basic flat knot. With an additional cord in the middle, this knot is arranged in a series of left-hand and right-hand flat knots, implying peace and prosperity forever. The application is very extensive, such as bracelets and belts.

Knot Type
Modified single knot

Suggested Materials
1 active cord: 2.5 mm (Dia.), 80 cm (L)
1 anchoring cord: 2.5 mm (Dia.), 30 cm (L)

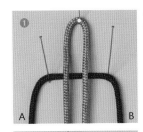
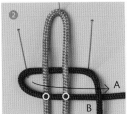
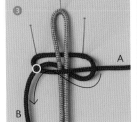
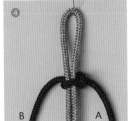

1 Pin the yellow anchoring cord in the middle. Place the center of the red cord under the yellow cord as a cross. The left side is A and the right is B. As shown, bend cords A & B 90° downwards. Set with pins. First is to make the left-hand flat knot. Turn cord A to the right over the yellow cord and under cord B. Take cord B to the left under the yellow cord, passing it through the left loop, and pull it out from the front. Remove the pins on the red cord and tighten the knot. The left-hand flat knot is done.

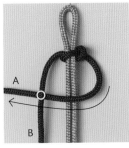
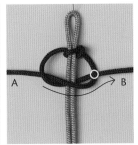
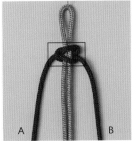

2 Next is to make the right-hand flat knot. Bend cord A on the right side to the left over the yellow cord and under cord B. Move cord B to the right under the yellow cord, passing it through the right loop, and pull it out from the front. Tighten the knot. This is the right-hand flat knot.
   A complete flat knot is a set of left-hand and right-hand flat knots. The binding of the left-hand flat knot is on the right side of the anchoring cord while that of the right-hand flat knot is on the left side. Repeat the left-hand and right-hand flat knots alternatively to form several sets of flat knots. Done!

Bracelet
Cords: 1 red cord, 2.5 mm (Dia.),
    200 cm (L); 1 yellow cord,
    2.5 mm (Dia.), 70 cm (L)

1 Produce a number of flat knot sets until it reaches the desired length. Ensure the size of the yellow loop on top is appropriate for a button knot.

2 Trim the ends of the red cord and seal them close to the knots with a flame.

3 Construct a button knot with the yellow cord. Trim the ends of the yellow cord. Seal them with a flame and conceal the joint in the button knot. Insert the button knot into the yellow loop. The bracelet is done!

20. Extended Flat Knot with Outer Loops

This knot is a variation of the extended flat knot. The basic construction is the same. You can choose the colors of the cords according to your design. For clearer demonstration, the example below is in 2 different colors.

Knot Type
Modified single knot

Suggested Materials
1 active cord: 2.5 mm (Dia.), 100 cm (L)
1 anchoring cord: 2.5 mm (Dia.), 20 cm (L)

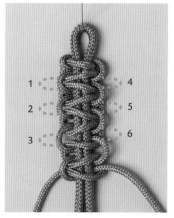

1 First is to make the extended flat knots. Do not tighten the knots. Identify the outer loops on both sides. They are in pairs and at the same level. The left loops are in the front and the right loops are at the back.

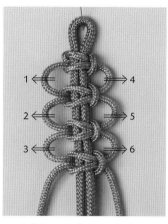

2 Pull the outer loops on both sides outwards at the same level.

3 Tighten the knots by pushing them upwards. Done!

Barrette
Cords: 1 dark yellow cord, 2.5 mm (Dia.), 100 cm (L); 1 orange cord, 2.5 mm (Dia.), 20 cm (L)
Finding: 1 metal barrette

1 Set the length of the anchoring cord in proportion to the barrette. Trim the ends and seal with a flame. Shift the joint so that it is concealed in the knots. Then continue to create more extended flat knots with outer loops.

2 As shown, trim the ends and seal them to the knots with a flame.

3 Attach the finished extended flat knots with outer loops to the barrette with hot glue. This is the finished product.

21. Twisted Flat Knot

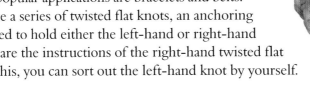

The twisted flat knot is derived from the basic flat knot. It has an auspicious implication of changing luck due to its twisting pattern. The popular applications are bracelets and belts.

To interlace a series of twisted flat knots, an anchoring cord is required to hold either the left-hand or right-hand knots. Below are the instructions of the right-hand twisted flat knots. From this, you can sort out the left-hand knot by yourself.

Knot Type
Modified single knot

Suggested Materials
1 active cord: 2.5 mm (Dia.), 80 cm (L)
1 anchoring cord: 2.5 mm (Dia.), 30 cm (L)

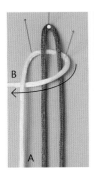 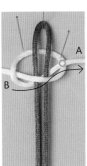 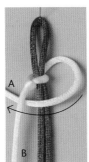 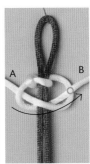  

Fold the pink anchoring cord in half and pin the middle. Place the middle of the multi-color cord under the pink cord and set with pins as shown. The left side is A and the right is B. First is to make the right-hand twisted flat knot. Move cord B to the left over the pink cord and under cord A. Then take cord A to the right under the pink cord and pull it out from the right loop. Tighten the knot. The right-hand twisted flat knot is done. Next is to make another right-hand twisted flat knot. Take cord A to the left over the pink cord and under cord B. Then bend cord B to the right under the pink cord and pull it out from the right loop. Tighten the knot. The bending edge is formed on the left side. Repeat the steps to form the twist.

Bracelet
Cords: 1 multi-color cord, 2.5 mm (Dia.), 200 cm (L); 1 pink cord, 2.5 mm (Dia.), 70 cm (L)

1 Continue to make the twisted flat knots until it reaches the desired bracelet length. Note that the pink loop on top is in proportion to a button knot.

2 Trim the multi-color cord ends and seal them to the bracelet with a flame. Then tie a button knot with the pink cord.

3 Trim the ends and seal with a flame. Tuck the joint into the knot. Finished.

Fig. 50   From left to right: extended flat knot and twisted flat knot bracelet with paired beads, multicolor twisted flat knot bracelet, extended flat knot bracelet, extended flat knot and twisted flat knot bracelet with porcelain beads.

Fig. 51   From left to right: clove hitch bracelet, snake knot bracelet with porcelain tube bead, *jingang* knot bracelet with jade beads, four-strand plait bracelet, dew knot charm with metal pendant.

22. Round Corn Knot

The corn knot is named after its shape and associated with fruitfulness and success. There are 2 types, round corn knot and square corn knot. When twining the corn knot, the cords can be the same or different colors. Here, the instructions are in 2 different colors for clearer demonstration.

The common applications of the round corn knot are pendants, bracelets, straps, and firecracker ornaments.

Knot Type
Traditional modified combination knot

Suggested Materials
2 cords: 2.5 mm (Dia.), 50 cm (L)

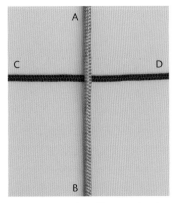

1 Place the red cord horizontal and lay the yellow cord on top in the center. Set with pins. The upper part of the yellow cord is A and the lower is B; the left side of the red cord is C and the right is D.

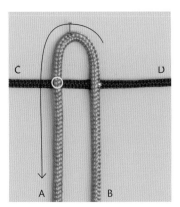

2 As shown, take cord A to the left and down to form a U-bend over the red cord.

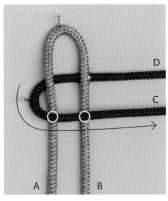

3 Take cord C down and to the right over the yellow cord to form another U-bend.

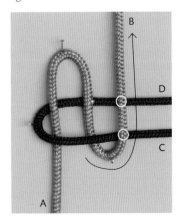

4 Take cord B to the right and up over the red cord to form 1 more U-bend.

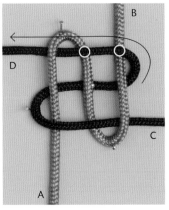

5 Move cord D up and to the left, going over-over-under the yellow cord. The base is set.

6 Next is shaping. Pull all the cord outwards to tighten. The first knot is done. Note that all cords are on the same level when pulling; otherwise the knot will be out of shape.

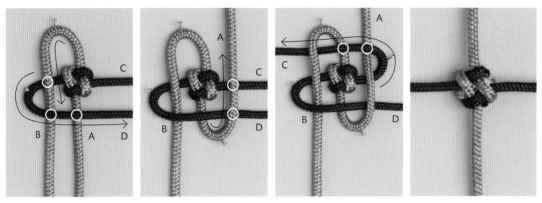

7 Repeat steps 2 to 6 to complete the 2nd layer.

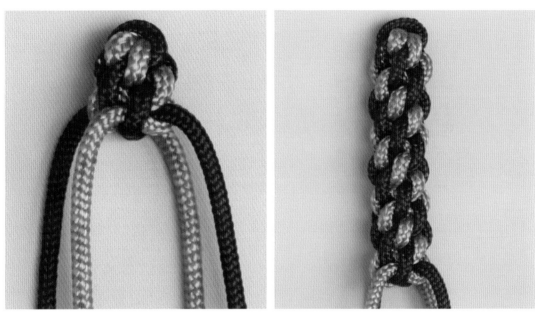

8 Continue to repeat steps 2 to 6 to form more layers. This is the round corn knot.

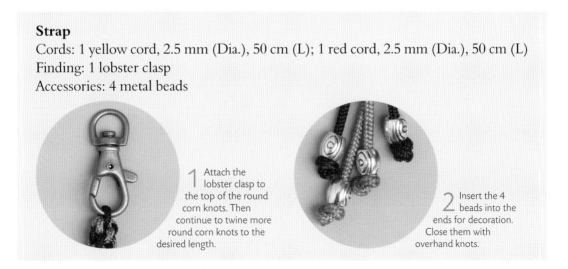

Strap

Cords: 1 yellow cord, 2.5 mm (Dia.), 50 cm (L); 1 red cord, 2.5 mm (Dia.), 50 cm (L)

Finding: 1 lobster clasp

Accessories: 4 metal beads

1 Attach the lobster clasp to the top of the round corn knots. Then continue to twine more round corn knots to the desired length.

2 Insert the 4 beads into the ends for decoration. Close them with overhand knots.

23. Square Corn Knot

The square corn knot is also a type of corn knot, commonly used as bracelets and decorations on clothes. Same as round corn knot, it requires 2 cords to complete and they can be the same or different color. Here, we have yellow and green cords for clearer demonstration.

Knot Type
Traditional modified combination knot

Suggested Materials
2 cords: 2.5 mm (Dia.), 50 cm (L)

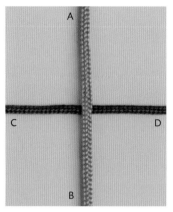

1 Place the green cord horizontally and set the yellow cord vertically on top, overlapping at the centers. The top part of the yellow cord is A and the lower is B; the left side of the green cord is C and the right is D.

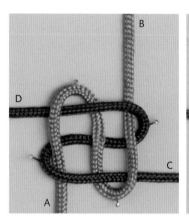

2 The 1st layer is the same as the round corn knot. Note that the arrangement is anticlockwise, i.e. cord A turns to the left and then downwards to form the 1st U-bend.

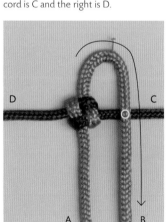

3 The 2nd layer is similar to the 1st but in a reverse configuration. Turn cord B clockwise to make a U-bend over cord C.

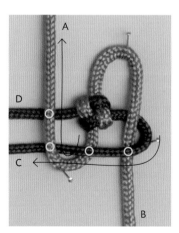

4 Bring cord C down and to the left to form another U-bend over the yellow cord. Take cord A to the left and up to form 1 more U-bend over the green cord.

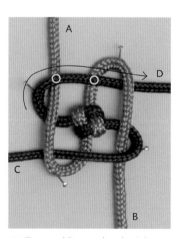

5 Turn cord D up and to the right, going over-over-under the yellow cord.

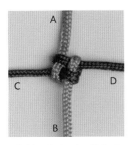

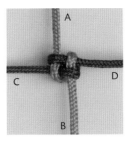

6 Next is shaping. Pull all the ends outwards to tighten the knot. The 2nd layer is done. Note that the 2nd layer is in a clockwise arrangement.

7 The 3rd layer is the same as the 1st layer, i.e. in an anticlockwise configuration.

8 The 4th layer is the same as the 2nd layer, i.e. in a clockwise arrangement.

9 Turn the knots downwards as shown in the figure. Continue to make more knots clockwise and anticlockwise in alternation to complete.

Comparison

The left figure is the round corn knot that is twined in 1 direction. The 2 cords of different colors are staggered.

The right figure is the square corn knot that is twined clockwise and anticlockwise in alternation. The 2 cords of different colors are in linear arrangement.

Round Corn Knot

Square Corn Knot

Corn Knot Earring

Cords: 1 yellow cord, 2.5 mm (Dia.), 50 cm (L); 1 green cord, 2.5 mm (Dia.), 50 cm (L)
Finding: 1 earing hook

1 Produce a series of corn knots to the desired length. Leave 2 mm at the cord ends and trim.

2 Seal the ends to the core with a flame. The main part of the earring is complete.

3 Attach an earring hook to the top. Hold both ends and twist to form a spiral shape. Done!

24. Cross Knot

The cross knot is one of the basic knots. It is named due to the shape. In Chinese, the cross shape looks the same as number ten (*shi*, 十), which has an auspicious meaning of perfect. The cross knot is very neat and easy to be twined, commonly combined with other knots or arranged in a series.

Knot Type
Basic single knot

Suggested Materials
1 cord: 2.5 mm (Dia.), 50 cm (L)

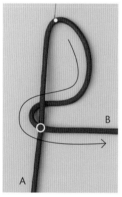

1 Pin the middle of the cord. The left side is A and the right is B. Move cord B to the left under cord A. Then turn it down and to the right over cord A.

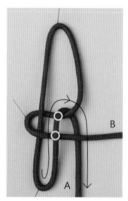

2 Take cord A to the right and up, going over the cord. Then turn it downwards under the cord.

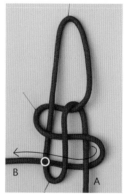

3 Turn cord B down and to the left, going under-under-over the cord. The base is set.

4 Pull the top loop and both ends to tighten the knot.

Earrings
Cords: 2 red cords, 2.5 mm (Dia.), 50 cm (L)
Findings: 2 earring hooks, 2 ribbon clamps, 2 jump rings
Accessories: 2 metal beads

2 If using method I, attach the ribbon clamp to conceal the cord ends. Add the jump ring and attach the earring hook to it. If using method II, attach the ribbon clamp to the tip of the loop. Add the jump ring and attach the earring hook to it.

1 There are 2 methods. Method I: Thread the metal bead on the cord. Then create a cross knot. Method II: create a cross knot first. Then add the metal bead. Trim and seal the ends together with a flame.

3 The left figure is the front of the earring and the right figure is the back. Repeat the steps to make another earring to complete the set.

25. Bowknot

A bowknot with a long tail looks like a little dragonfly. With its aesthetic and functional characteristics, the bowknot is commonly used to tie the strings of the ancient Chinese instrument—*guqin*.

Knot Type
Modified single knot

Suggested Materials
1 cord: 2 mm (Dia.), 30 cm (L)

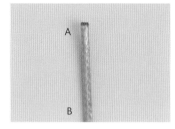

1 Place the cord vertically. The top part is A and the bottom is B.

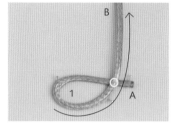

2 Take cord B to the left and turn anticlockwise to form a loop under the cord. Set with a pin. This is loop 1.

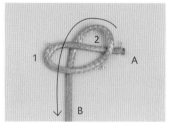

3 Bring cord A down, going under loop 1 to form loop 2. Now the loops are overlapping.

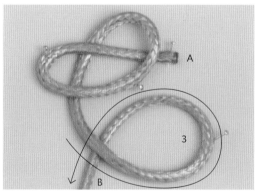

4 Take the bottom cord A to the right and curve it anticlockwise to form a bigger loop under the cord. This is loop 3.

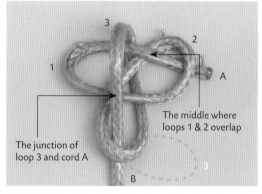

The middle where loops 1 & 2 overlap

The junction of loop 3 and cord A

5 Hold the junction of loop 3 and cord A, and turn loop 3 90° anticlockwise. Then wrap loop 3 around loops 1 & 2, and set it in the middle where loops 1 & 2 overlap. The base is done.

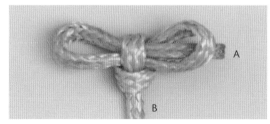

6 Tighten the knot by pulling cord B downwards. Adjust the loops symmetrically. The bowknot is complete. The left figure is the front and the right figure is the back.

26. Chain Knot

The chain knot is easy to learn and very practical. The common applications are bracelets and necklaces.

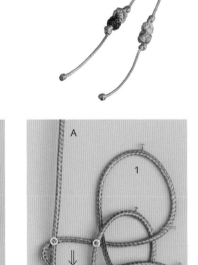

Knot Type
Modified single knot

Suggested Materials
1 cord: 2.5 mm (Dia.), 50 cm (L)

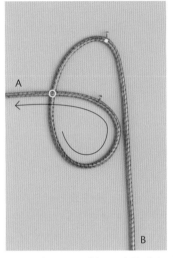

1 Pin the center of the cord. The left side is A and the right is B. Take cord A to the right and turn anticlockwise over the upper part of cord A to form a loop. Set with a pin.

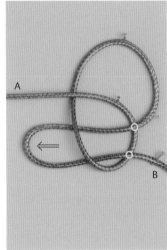

2 Form a U-bend with cord B. Pass it through the loop, going over and under. Set with pins.

3 Form a U-bend with cord A and insert it into the horizontal U-bend from the top. The base is set. For easy reference, let's call the top loop 1 and the bottom loop 2.

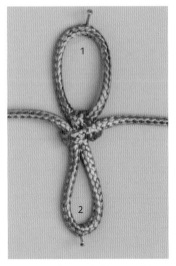

4 Next is shaping. Pull loops 1 & 2 together with the ends to tighten the knot.

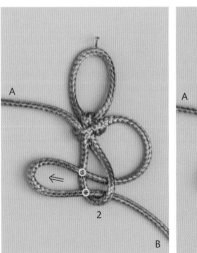

5 Form a U-bend with cord B and insert it into loop 2 from the right. Pull end A to close loop 2. Loop 3 is formed.

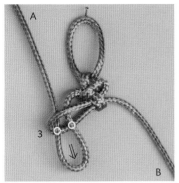
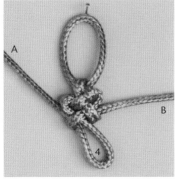

6 Make a U-bend with cord A and insert it into loop 3 from the top. Pull cord B to close loop 3. Loop 4 is formed.

7 Repeat steps 5 & 6 until it reached the desired length.

8 To close the ends, insert the left cord end into the loop. Then insert the right cord end into the same loop. Tighten to complete.

Decorative Pendant

Cords: 1 yellow cord, 2.5 mm (Dia.), 100 cm (L); 1 pink cord, 1 purple cord, 1 blue cord, 1 green cord, 2.5 mm (Dia.), 50 cm (L)

1 Thread the yellow cord through the pierced item to be decorated. Then create a binding knot and a series of chain knots until the desired length is reached.

2 Make a multiple overhand knot a bit away the end of the chain knot. Thread 2 pineapple knots of different colors on the cord and make another multiple overhand knot to position the pineapple knots. Do the same for the other cord.

3 Create an overhand knot a bit away from the multiple overhand knot. Trim and seal the end with a flame. Do the same for the other side. The decorative pendant is done.

27. Double-Connection Knot

The double-connection knot is one of the most popular basic single knots. It has an implication of connecting continuously since "connect" in Chinese is a homophone of "continue" (*lian*). This knot is compact and firm, not easy to be deformed. Because of the durability, it is commonly used in positioning the main knots, tying the cord ends, making belts, bracelets, and necklaces.

Knot Type
Basic single knot

Suggested Materials
1 cord: 2.5 mm (Dia.), 50 cm (L)

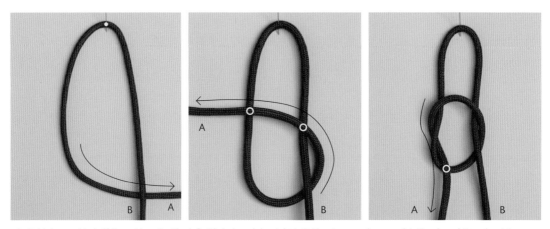

1 Fold the cord in half. Set with a pin. The left side is A and the right is B. First is to work on cord A. Bend cord A to the right, going under cord B. Then move it to the upper left and over the cord. Turn it downwards as shown, passing under and over the loop. Pull and adjust as shown in the figure.

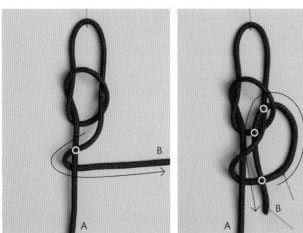

2 Next is to work on cord B. Bend cord B to the left over cord A. Then wrap around cord A and turn anticlockwise passing the loops to form another loop as shown. The base is done.

3 Next is shaping. Pull gently to tighten the knot. Done!

Small Pendant

Cord: 1 red cord, 2.5 mm
(Dia.), 50 cm (L)
Finding: 1 key ring or 1
lobster clasp
Accessories: 2 beads

Trim the ends of the double-connection knot to the desired length. Insert the beads and make the multiple overhand knots, one at each end. Add a key ring or a lobster clasp on top.

Peace Necklace

Cords : 2 green cords, 2 mm (Dia.), 110 cm (L)
Findings: 2 cord end caps, 2 jump rings
Accessories: 1 pierced jade disc, 1 silver lotus seed pod charm, 4 silver endless knot charms, 2 silver oval beads, 4 silver spacer beads, 2 silver lotus charms

1 Thread the silver lotus seed pod charm on the cord and place it on the center of the jade disc. Tie together the charm and the jade disc with the other cord by making a cross binding knot. Then create a double-connection knot, insert the endless knot charm, make 2 double-connection knots with space in between, insert the silver oval bead, and make another double-connection knot. Do the same on the other side. The front part of the necklace is done.

2 Create a double-connection knot 3 cm away from the last knot. Insert the endless knot charm, make 2 double-connection knots with space in between, insert the silver spacer bead, create another double-connection knot, insert another silver spacer bead, and tie one more double-connection knot.

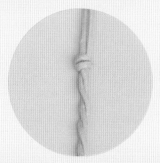

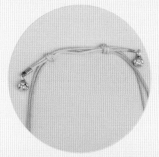

3 Then twist the 2 cords and set with a double-conection knot. The double-connection knots here are not only decorative but also positioning the beads and charms.

4 Attach the cord end cap to the cord ends and fasten the silver lotus charm with the jump ring to the end cap. Do the same on the other side. Lastly, create a sliding knot and adjust the length. The necklace is done.

28. Horizontal Double-Connection Knot

Arrange the horizontal double-connection knots in a series to form a loop-chain that can be used as belts, bracelets, and necklaces.

Knot Type
Modified single knot

Suggested Materials
1 cord: 2.5 mm (Dia.), 50 cm (L)

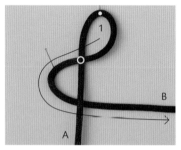
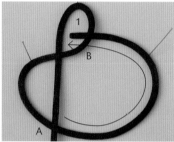
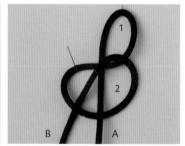

1 Fold the cord in half and pin at the middle. The left side is A and the right is B. Take cord B down and turn to the left over cord A to form loop 1. Take cord B down and to the right under cord A. Then move it up, turn anticlockwise, and pull it out from loop 1. This is loop 2 with cord A in the middle, dividing the loop into left and right. Take cord B to the lower left over the intersection of loops 1 & 2 and pull it out from the back of the left loop 2.

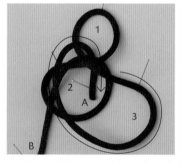
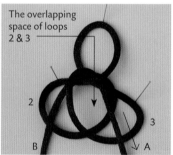
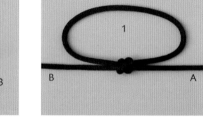

2 Take cord A to the right over the right loop 2. Then turn it down and clockwise, passing it through loop 1 from the front to form loop 3. Bring cord A out from the overlapping space of loops 2 & 3. The base is set.

3 Pull simultaneously cord B on the left side with the left side of loop 1 to the left, and cord A on the right side with the right side of loop 1 to the right until the knot is tightened. Done.

Bracelet
Cord: 1 red cord, 2.5 mm (Dia.), 100 cm (L)
Finding: 1 cord end cap
Accessory: 1 silver lotus seed pod charm

1 First is to create a cross knot. Then make a series of horizontal double-connection knots until the desired length is reached.

2 Attach the cord end cap to enclose the ends. Then add the silver lotus seed pod.

3 The bracelet is complete.

29. Single-Loop Double-Connection Knot

This knot is a variation of the double-connection knot. It is small and neat, commonly used for decorations and setting other knots.

The difference between the double-connection knot and the single-loop double-connection knot is the position of the cord ends when the knots are completed. The ends of the double-connection knot are gathered on one side, whereas those of the single-loop double-connection knot are separated to both sides. There is also an outer loop on the side.

Knot Type
Modified single knot

Suggested Materials
1 cord: 2.5 mm (Dia.), 40 cm (L)

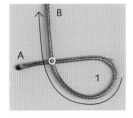

1 Pin the cord 10 cm from the left. Turn cord B clockwise over cord A. Loop 1 is formed.

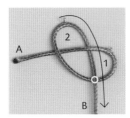

2 Continue to turn cord B clockwise, going under and over loop 1. This is loop 2.

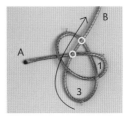

3 Keep turning cord B clockwise, passing through loop 1 from the back to form loop 3.

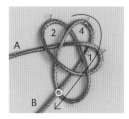

4 Take cord B to the lower left, going under loop 2, and pull it out from loop 3 to form loop 4.

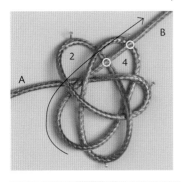

5 Take cord B to the upper right and pull it out from the intersection of loops 1, 2 & 4. The base is set.

6 Tighten the knot by pulling loop 3 and the cord ends. Adjust the size of loop 3. The knot is complete. The upper figure is the front and the lower figure is the back. The cross knot in the middle is the symbol of the double-connection knot.

Earing
Cord: 1 green cord,
 2.5 mm (Dia.), 50 cm (L)
Findings: 1 earring hook,
 1 head pin, 1 floral
 bead cap
Accessory: 1 bead

1 Create 2 single-loop double-connection knots with certain space in between.

2 Fold the middle of the cord between the 2 knots. Pass both cord ends through the bead.

3 Trim and flame the ends to position the bead. Attach the earring hook between the 2 single-loop double-connection knots. Attach the floral bead cap at the bottom of the bead and insert the head pin needle to set.

30. Flat Square Knot

The flat square knot is simple and neat, indicating integrity, commonly used as ornaments and means of connection.

Knot Type
Modified single knot

Suggested Materials
1 cord: 2.5 mm (Dia.), 50 cm (L)

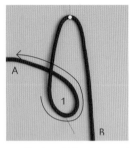
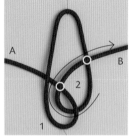
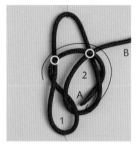
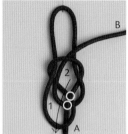

1 Pin the middle of the cord. The left side is A and the right is B. Take cord A to the right and turn it anticlockwise under the upper part of cord A. Loop 1 is formed. Move cord B to the left, pulling it through loop 1 from the front. Take it clockwise to the upper right over the upper part of cord B to form loop 2. The 2 loops are now interlocking.

2 Take cord A to the right, going over the middle part of the cord. Wrap it around the right side of loop 2 and pull end A from the front. Then take it over the intersection of the loops and pass through loop 1 from the front.

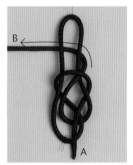

3 Move cord B to the left under the top U-bend. Then take it down to go over-under-over-under the loops. The base is set.

4 Pull gently the top loop together with both ends to tighten the knot. The flat square knot is complete.

Earring
Cord: 1 red cord,
　　2.5 mm (Dia.),
　　50 cm (L)
Findings: 1 earring
　　hook, 1 jump ring
Accessories: 2 silver
　　beads

1 Pass the cord through the jump ring of the earring hook. Then create a flat square knot below.

2 Insert the silver beads into the ends, one at each side. Trim the ends to the desired length and seal with a flame so that the beads do not fall out.

31. Double-Coin Knot

The double-coin knot is one of the oldest knots. The name comes from the pattern which looks like two overlapping coins.

In the old days, coin was the symbol of wealth. It also had the function of exorcising the evil spirits. In Chinese, "coin" is a homophone of "complete," which is commonly used in the auspicious tradition. Double-coin knot, therefore, has the symbolic meanings of wealth, exorcising the evil spirits, blessing, and propitiousness.

The shape of double-coin knot is neat and symmetrical. The formation is very flexible, which can be weaved horizontally, vertically, and braided with extra cords. It can be used individually as a decorative element or combined with other knots. For long term use, sew the back of the intersections to prevent the knot from changing the shape. Sewing a double-coin knot on a napkin is a way to provide an enhancement.

Knot Type
Basic single knot

Suggested Materials
1 cord: 2.5 mm (Dia.), 50 cm (L)

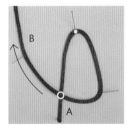

1 Pin one end of the cord on the board. Bend it as a U shape and set with pins. The cord end A is on the left and end B on the right. Move end B upwards and over end A. Set with pins.

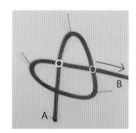

2 Bend end B towards the right and over the cord. Set with pins.

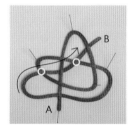

3 Move end B downwards and under end A. Move end B towards the top right, going under-over-under-over the cord sections. This is the base.

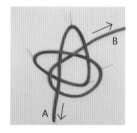

4 Next is shaping. Remove the pins and pull both ends of the cord.

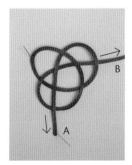

5 Refer to the figure of step 6 when pulling to adjust the shape. Do not over pull. Leave some space in between.

6 The double-coin knot is complete. Be sure the knot is symmetrical and the 3 circular overlapping sections are smooth.

Napkin Decoration
Cord: 1 red cord, 2.5mm (Dia.), 50cm (L)

1 Trim the excess and leave enough ends to form a loop. Seal the ends with a flame. Move the joint until it is over another section of the cord.

2 Turn over the knot and the joint is hidden.

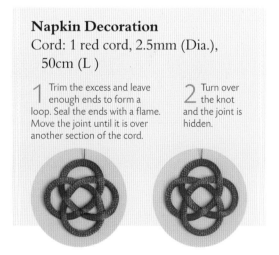

32. Vertical Double-Coin Knot

This is another common type of double-coin knot, which can be assembled from the left or right. The horizontal double-coin knot discussed earlier is mainly arranged by using one side of the cord; however, this vertical double-coin knot is formed by intertwining both sides of the cord. It is often used to make long bracelets and belts.

Knot Type
Basic single knot

Suggested Materials
1 cord: 4 mm (W), 80 cm (L)

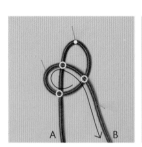 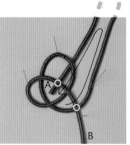 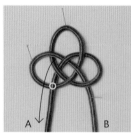 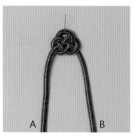

1 First is to make the right-sided vertical double-coin knot. Pin the middle of the cord on the board. The left side is A and the right is B. Pull end B to the left and bend clockwise to form a loop over the cord. Move end A upwards over cord B. Set with pins. Move end A to the lower left, going under and over loops, then under and over again. Pull end A and adjust to complete this first knot.

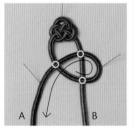  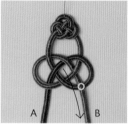 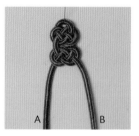

2 Next is to form a left-sided vertical double-coin knot below. Pull end A to the right and loop anti-clockwise over the cord. Set with pins. Move end B towards the upper left over end A. Then bend end B downwards, going under and over the first loop, and under and over again. Pull end B and adjust to form this second knot. Continue to create more knots until the desired length is reached.

Barrette
Cord: 1 purple flat cord, 4 mm (W), 80 cm (L)
Finding: 1 metal barrette

1 Make several vertical double-coin knots until the desired length is reached. Trim the ends reserving enough to form a loop.

2 Seal the ends with a flame. Move the joint until it is over another junction of the cord. This is the back of the accessory.

3 Choose a metal barrette that is shorter and narrower than the knot. Use hot glue to attach the back side of the knots onto the barrette. Done!

33. Long Double-Coin Knot

The long double-coin knot is a variation of a double-coin knot. It is a series of double-coin knot extending vertically, implying wealthy forever. Here, we will introduce the technique of using 1 cord. You can also produce the knots with 2 or 4 cords. Long double-coin knot is good for hair accessories, belts, bookmarks, and cell phone pendants.

Knot Type
Modified single knot

Suggested Materials
1 cord: 3 mm (W), 100 cm (L)

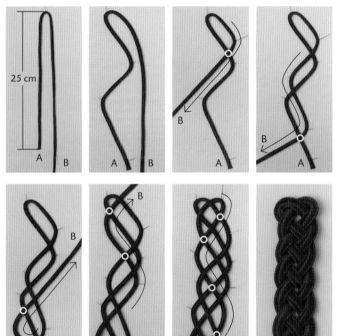

1 Pin the cord at ¼ of the length from the left. The left side is A and the right is B. Cord A is approximately 25 cm and B is approximately 75 cm. In the 2nd figure, bend cord A to form a Z shape. Set with pins. The following steps are done by twinning cord B. Cord B goes downwards. First, bend cord B 90° to the lower left over the upper part of the Z shape. Next, bend cord B 90° to the lower right under the middle Z, and turn it 90° to the lower left over the lower Z. Set with pins. You can find that cord B runs the same direction as cord A and the right angles of cord B are diagonally above those of cord A.

2 In the 1st and 2nd figures, cord B moves upwards. First, bend cord B to the right, going over and under the loops. Then turn 90° to the upper left, going under and over the loops. Again, turn 90° to the upper right, going over and under the loops. Set with pins. You can find that the movement of cord B is similar to cord A and the right angles of cord B are diagonally below those of cord A. In the 3rd figure, cord B goes downwards. First, bend cord B to the lower left, going over-under-over the loops. Turn 90° to the lower right, going under-over-under the loops. Then, turn 90° to the lower left, going over-under-over the loops. Set with pins. The base of the knot is done. Next is to adjust the shape as shown in the 4th figure. Pull the cord to tighten the knot. It's complete.

Bookmark
Cords: 1 red flat cord, 4 mm (W), 100 cm (L); 1 orange cord, 1.5 mm (Dia.), 20 cm (L)

1 Reserve enough cord ends to form a loop and trim. Seal the ends with a flame.

2 Move the joint until it is covered by another section of the cord. The figure is the front.

3 Take an approximately 20-cm-long orange cord and form 2 figure-eight knots, one at each end. Attach the orange cord to the long double-coin knot by making a binding knot. The bookmark is finished!

34. Compound Double-Coin Knot

The compound double-coin knot is a variation of double-coin knot. It is prepared by two cords and well-suited to make long knot ornaments. You can choose different colors according to your design.

Knot Type
Modified single knot

Suggested materials
2 cords: 3 mm (Dia.), 55 cm (L)

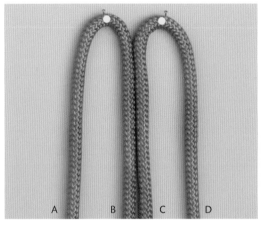

1 Pin the centers of the cords. The left side of the left cord is A and the right side is B. The left side of the right cord is C and the right side is D. Be sure cords B and C are set parallel and close to each other.

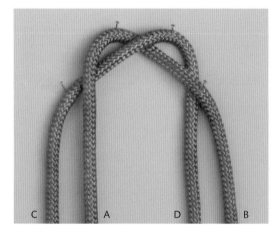

2 Take cord C over cord B and under cord A. Move cord B over cord D.

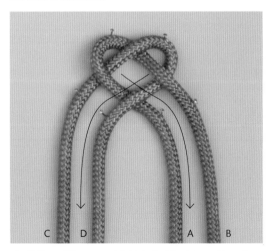

3 Shift cord D over cord A. Note that the intersection of cords A & D are perpendicularly below that of cords B & C.

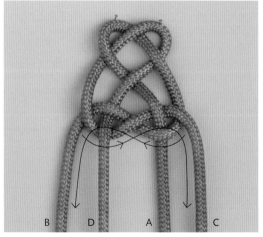

4 Take cord C to the right, going under cords A & D, then over cord B. Let cord C hang down. Move cord B to the left, going over-under-over-under the other cords. Let cord B hang down. The first set of knots is done.

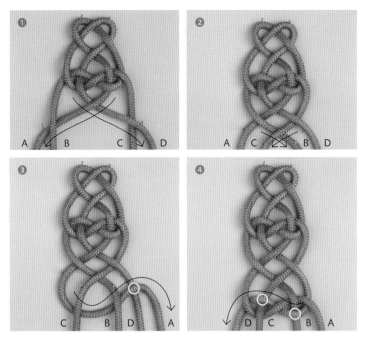

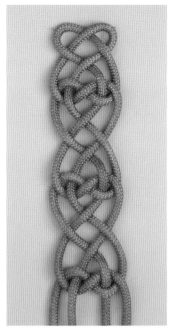

5 Repeat steps 2 to 4 to complete the second set of knots.

6 Repeat the same steps to produce more sets of knots until the desired length is reached. Adjust to make them symmetrical. Done!

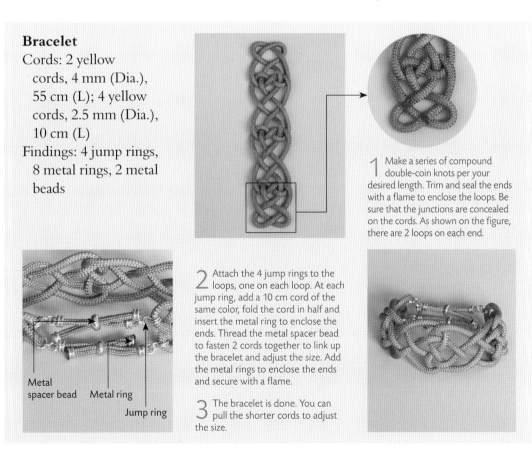

Bracelet

Cords: 2 yellow
cords, 4 mm (Dia.),
55 cm (L); 4 yellow
cords, 2.5 mm (Dia.),
10 cm (L)
Findings: 4 jump rings,
8 metal rings, 2 metal
beads

1 Make a series of compound double-coin knots per your desired length. Trim and seal the ends with a flame to enclose the loops. Be sure that the junctions are concealed on the cords. As shown on the figure, there are 2 loops on each end.

Metal spacer bead   Metal ring   Jump ring

2 Attach the 4 jump rings to the loops, one on each loop. At each jump ring, add a 10 cm cord of the same color, fold the cord in half and insert the metal ring to enclose the ends. Thread the metal spacer bead to fasten 2 cords together to link up the bracelet and adjust the size. Add the metal rings to enclose the ends and secure with a flame.

3 The bracelet is done. You can pull the shorter cords to adjust the size.

35. Two-Outer-Loop Double-Coin Knot

This is another variation of a double-coin knot. The configuration of the two-outer-loop double-coin knot is very neat and decent, representing harmony. This is commonly used in celebrations as pendants and gifts.

Knot Type
Modified single knot

Suggested Materials
1 cord: 3 mm (Dia.), 80 cm (L)

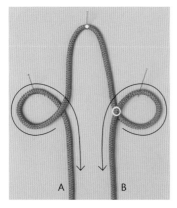

1 Pin the center of the cord. The left side is A and the right is B. Move cord B to the right. Loop anticlockwise over the upper part of cord B. Then move cord A to the left. Loop clockwise under the upper part of cord A.

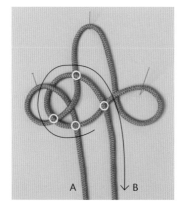

2 Bend cord B to the left, going over the end of cord A, then over and under the loop of cord A. Continue to bend clockwise over both cord A and B as shown.

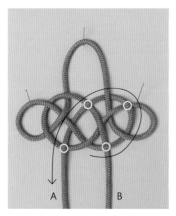

3 Next is to twine cord A. Bend cord A to the right, going over the end of cord B, then under and over the loop of cord B. Continue to bend cord A to the lower left, going under the upper part of cord B, then over-under-over the loops as shown. This forms the base of the knot.

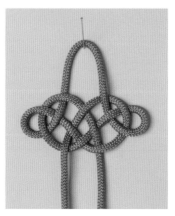

4 Adjust accordingly. Note that this is a symmetrical piece with proper spacing. Done!

Pendant
Cord: 1 yellow
    cord, 4 mm (Dia.),
    80 cm (L)
Accessories: 2 tassels

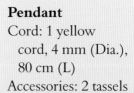

Add tassels at both ends. This can be hung up as a pendant ornament.

36. Three-Outer-Loop Double-Coin Knot

The three-outer-loop double-coin knot is a traditional variation knot. In Buddhism, it is a symbol of solemnness and often used as ornaments in temples. Other applications are pendants and gift decorations.

Knot Type
Modified single knot

Suggested Materials
1 cord: 2.5 mm (Dia.), 80 cm (L)

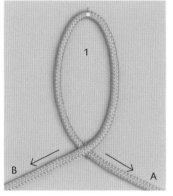

1 Pin the middle of the cord. The left side is A and the right is B. As shown, move cord B to the left overlapping cord A to form loop 1.

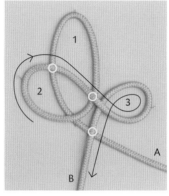

2 Take cord B upwards and turn clockwise over loop 1 to form loop 2. Then move it to the right and turn anticlockwise under the upper part of cord B to form a smaller loop (loop 3). Set with pins. Take end B over cord A.

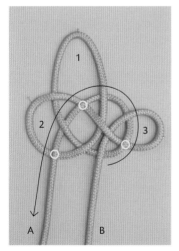

3 Move cord A to the right, going anticlockwise over and under loop 3. Then pass it under the right side of loop 1, going over-under-over loops 1 & 2.

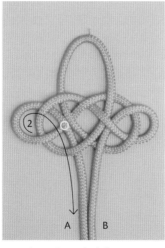

4 Take cord A to the left, going clockwise under-over-under loop 2. The base is set. Pull both ends to adjust the shape symmetrically with proper spacing. The knot is complete.

Pendant
Cord: 1 yellow cord, 4 mm (Dia.), 80 cm (L)
Accessory: 1 tassel

First is to make a three-outer-loop double-coin knot. Tie a double-connection knot with the ends. Then attach a tassel below.

37. Prosperity Knot

As described by its name, people believe that the prosperity knot is a lucky charm. Thus it is commonly seen in weddings and on women's accessories. To make the knot more interesting, extra cords can be added.

Knot Type
Modified single knot

Suggested Materials
1 cord: 2.5 mm (Dia.), 80 cm (L)

1 Pin the cord in the middle. The left side is A and the right is B.

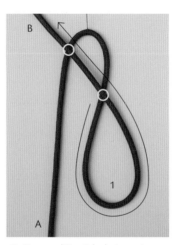

2 Turn cord B anticlockwise, going over the upper part of cord B and cord A. Loop 1 is formed.

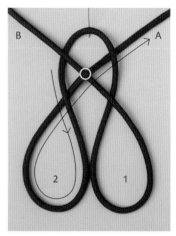

3 Turn cord A clockwise, going under-over-under the cord. Loop 2 is formed.

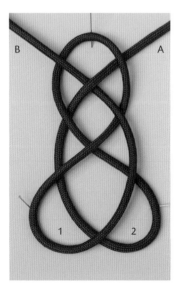

4 Shift loop 1 to the left and loop 2 to the right so that loop 1 overlaps loop 2.

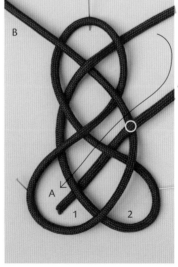

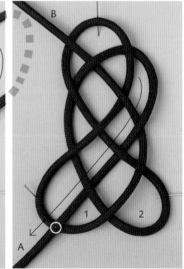

5 Take cord A clockwise to the lower left, going over-under-under-over the loops.

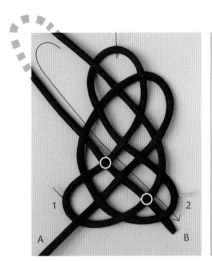  

6 Take cord B anticlockwise to the lower right, going under-over-under-over-under the loops. The base is set.

7 Pull the ends gently to shape the knot with proper spacing. The prosperity knot is complete.

Prosperity Bracelet
Cord: 1 red cord, 2.5 mm (Dia.), 300 cm (L)

1 First is to make a fastener. Create a loop on one end with a double-connection knot. Be sure that the loop is appropriate for the button knot in step 3.

2 Make 5 sets of cloverleaf knots and prosperity knots.

3 Last, form the 6th cloverleaf knot and end with a button knot. Insert the loop into the button knot to link it up. The prosperity bracelet is complete.

Hair Pin
This hair pin barrette is in a warm tone which is desireable to be used in winter time.

Cords: 1 red flat cord, 4 mm (W), 100 cm (L); 1 yellow flat cord, 4 mm (W), 100 cm (L); 1 brown flat cord, 4 mm (W), 100 cm (L)
Finding: 1 silver hair pin

Create a prosperity knot with the red cord. Following the same path, triple the knot with the yellow and brown cords. Trim and seal the ends together with a flame. Conseal the joints by shifting them behind the intersections. Insert the silver pin. The barrette is complete.

38. Extended Prosperity Knot

The extended prosperity knot is derived from the prosperity knot. It is commonly used to create belts, bracelets, and decorations for bags and hats.

Knot Type
Modified single knot

Suggested Materials
1 cord: 2.5 mm (Dia.), 90 cm (L)

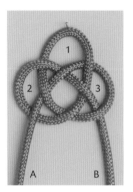

1 Make a double-coin knot.

2 Pull loops 2 & 3 outwards, shaping them into ovals.

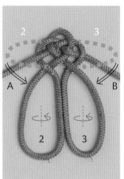

3 As shown in the figure, bring loop 2 down and flip to the right so that the left cord is on top. Then bring loop 3 down and flip to the right so that the left cord is on top.

Pull loop 2 out from the center of loop 3 and adjust as shown in the figure.

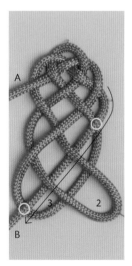

5 Move cord B from the right to the lower left, going over-under-under-over the loops.

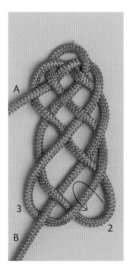

6 Refer to the figure, bring the tip of loop 2 backwards, going under loop 3.

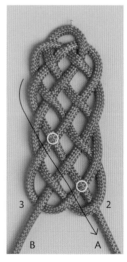

7 Take cord A to the lower right, going under-over-under-over-under the loops. The base is set.

8 Adjust the shape according to the figure with proper spacing. The knot is done! Attach the extended prosperity knot onto the wallet strap closure.

39. Cicada Wing Knot

The name of cicada wing knot is derived from its shape. In Chinese culture, cicada represents everlasting. This knot is small and commonly used for gift wrapping.

Knot Type
Modified single knot

Suggested Materials
1 cord: 3.5 mm (W), 50 cm (L)

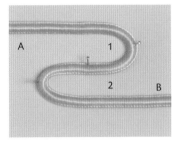

1 As shown on the figure, bend the cord in S shape. Set with pins. The top is cord A and loop 1, whereas the bottom is cord B and loop 2.

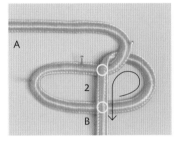

2 Take cord B anticlockwise, going under-over-over loop 2, and set it downwards.

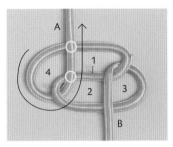

3 Take cord A clockwise, going under-over-over loop 2, and set it upwards. 4 loops are formed.

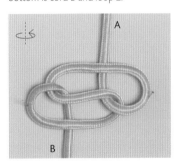

4 Flip it horizontally. Now cord A is on the upper right and cord B is on the below left.

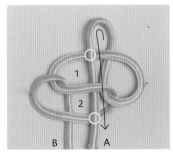

5 Take cord A anticlockwise and downwards, going over-under-over loops 1 and 2.

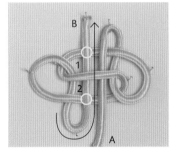

6 Move cord B anticlockwise and upwards, going over-under-over loops 2 and 1. Set it parallel to the left side of cord A. The base is set.

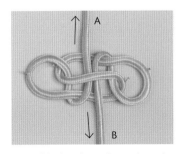

7 Pull both ends gently to tighten the knot.

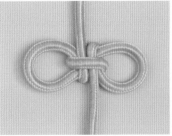
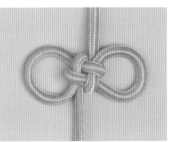

8 Adjust the loop and make it symmetrical. The cicada wing knot is done. The left figure is the front and the right figure is the back. Wrap the ends around the gift box. Adjust the position of the loops to from an attractive composition.

40. Pineapple Knot

The pineapple knot is a variation of a double-coin knot. It is 3-dimensional like a sphere, which has an implication of keeping the money rolling in. The application of the pineapple knot is flexible. It can be combined with beads to create bracelets, necklaces and pendants.

Knot Type
Modified single knot

Suggested Materials
1 cord: 2.5 mm (Dia.), 80 cm (L)

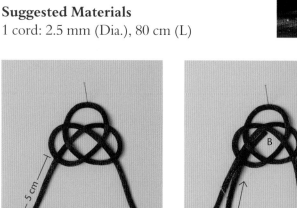

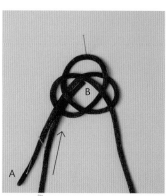

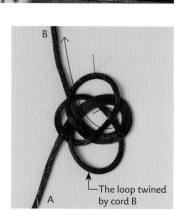

1 First is to make a double-coin knot. The 2 ends are in different lengths. The left is A, which is about 5 cm, leaving end B longer.

2 Move end B to the left and up, following the path of cord A on the inner side.

3 When twining cord B, the loop below has to be the same size as the upper loop. Continue to follow the path of cord A, passing the inner side of the right loop, as presented in the figure.

The loop twined by cord B

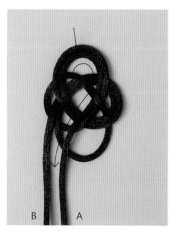

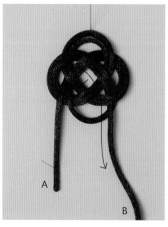

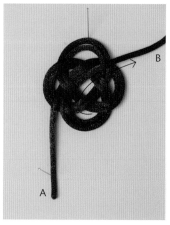

4 Continue to follow the route as shown, passing along the inner side of the upper loop.

5 Continue to follow the route as shown, passing along the inner side of the left loop.

6 Continue to follow the route as shown, passing along the inner side of the lower loop. The base is done.

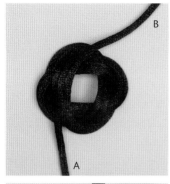

The cord end

7 Next is shaping. First, pull both ends from the middle so that the center is higher, forming a hemisphere. Continue to pull gently to tighten the knot until it forms a sphere.

8 Cut one end and seal it with a flame so that it stays inside the knot.

9 Repeat the same step to conceal the other end. The pineapple knot is finished. The left figure is the top view, which shows a hole in the middle for a cord or other material to go through. The right figure is the side view.

Earring

Cord: 1 red cord, 2.5 mm (Dia.), 80 cm (L)

Finding: 1 earing hook

Push the earring hook through the hole in the middle of the knot. It's done!

Pendant

You can attach the pineapple knots to other pendant as decoration.

First is to make several pineapple knots in different colors. String them with a cord and create a multiple overhand knot at the bottom to keep them in place.

41. Turtle Shell Knot

The turtle shell knot looks like the pattern and shape of the turtle shell; hence the name. The turtle connotes longevity in China. It is commonly used to make coasters and pendants.

Knot Type
Modified single knot

Suggested Materials
1 cord: 3.5 mm (W), 60 cm (L)

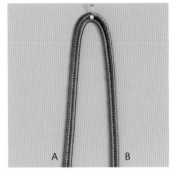

1 Pin the middle of the cord. The left side is A and the right is B.

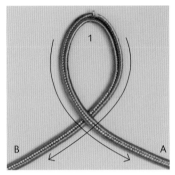

2 Move cord A over cord B to form loop 1.

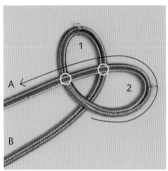

3 Turn cord A anticlockwise over loop 1. Loop 2 is formed.

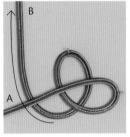

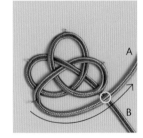

4 Take cord B upwards under cord A. Then turn it clockwise, going under-over-under-under loops 1 & 2. Loop 3 is formed.

5 Take cord A to the upper right over cord B. Then turn it anticlockwise, going over-under-over-over loop 2 and the upper part of cord A. Loop 4 is formed.

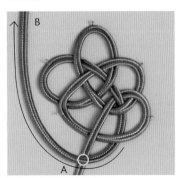

6 Take cord B to the upper left over cord A. Then turn it clockwise, going under-over-under-over-under-over loops 3 & 4. Loop 5 is formed.

7 Pull both ends and adjust the knot symmetrically. Done!

Turtle Pendant
Cords: 1 green flat cord, 3.5 mm (W), 100 cm (L); 2 green flat cords, 3.5 mm (W), 12 cm (L)
Finding: 1 cellphone strap
Accessory: 1 thick silver bead

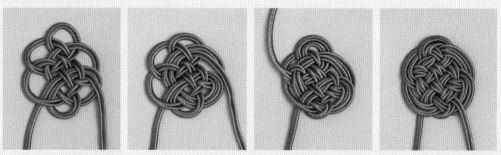

1 First is to make a turtle shell knot. Then double the knot by taking the right cord to go around the inner side of the original knot.

2 Form a button knot with the cord ends. This is the turtle head.

3 Next is to create the turtle legs. Seal one of the shorter cords together with a flame to form a circle. Push the middle of the circle together to form 2 equal loops. Do the same with the other cord.

4 Tuck the legs into the turtle shell knot diagonally to form a cross as shown. The little turtle is done. The left figure is the back and the right figure is the front.

5 Thread the thick silver bead on the cord above the button knot. Trim and seal the ends together with a flame. Attach the cellphone strap to the silver bead.

6 The pendant is complete.

42. Basket Knot

The basket knot is like a piece of fine weave that can be interlaced to different sizes. Due to its flexibility and durability, this knot is often used for practical items, such as coasters. You can choose different cord colors to present your creativity.

Knot Type
Modified single knot

Suggested Materials
1 cord: 3.5 cm (W), 150 cm (L)

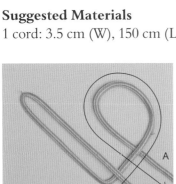 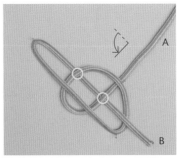 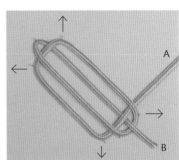

1 Make a U-bend as shown in the figure with the opening facing the lower right. Set with pins. The top part of the cord is B and the bottom part is A, which is the active cord. Take cord A to the upper right under cord B. Bend cord A anticlockwise to create a loop. Then turn the loop 90° anticlockwise, going over and under the U-bend. Stretch the loop in 4 directions to form a rectangle as shown.

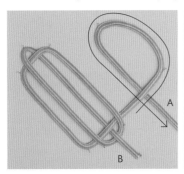 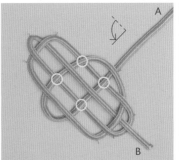 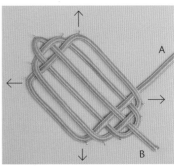

2 Bend cord A anticlockwise to form another loop. Again, turn the loop 90° anticlockwise, going over-under-over-under the loops. Then stretch the loop in 4 directions to form a rectangle as shown.

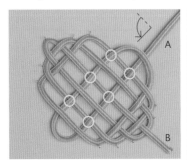 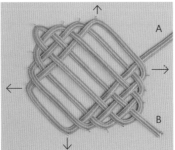 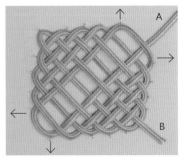

3 Repeat the same steps to extend the basket weave pattern.

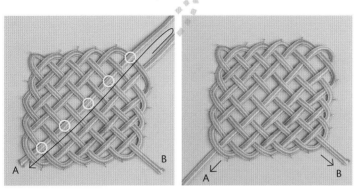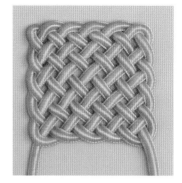

4 Take cord A to the lower left, going 5 times over and under the loops. Pull out cord end A.

5 Pull both ends to tighten the knot to form a square. Adjust the loops so that they are evenly distributed. The basket knot is done.

Coaster
Cord: 1 yellow flat cord, 3.5 cm (W), 150 cm (L)

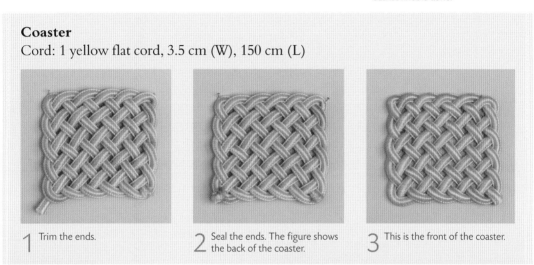

1 Trim the ends.

2 Seal the ends. The figure shows the back of the coaster.

3 This is the front of the coaster.

Fig. 52 Use various color cords with the supplementary cording technique to produce durable and beautiful basket knot coasters.

43. Sauvastika Knot

The sauvastika knot is one of the most popular basic single knots. The pattern is the same as the Buddhist symbol 卍, which represents prosperity and complete. This is the reason why the sauvastika knot is broadly adopted in Chinese ornaments. We will demonstrate how easy to make sauvastika knots and incorporate them with other elements.

Knot Type
Basic single knot

Suggested Materials
1 cord: 2.5 mm (Dia.), 50 cm (L)

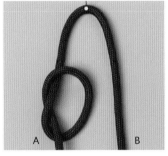

1 Fold the cord in half and pin the middle. The left side is A and the right is B. Bend cord A anticlockwise over the cord to form a loop as shown.

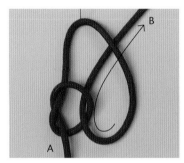

2 Bend cord B clockwise, passing through the left loop, and going under the top part of cord B. Then bring it down to form a loop as shown.

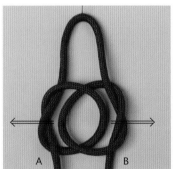

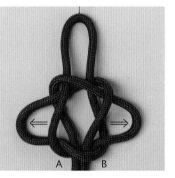

3 Pull the right side of the left loop through the overlapping area of the right loop to form a outer loop. Then pull the left side of the right loop through the overlapping area of the left loop to form another outer loop. Now you have 3 outer loops. The base is set.

4 Next is shaping. Pull the right and left outer loops outwards to tighten the knot. Adjust symmetrically.

Knotting Ornament
Cord: 1 red cord, 2.5 mm (Dia.), 50 cm (L)
Findings: 2 silver beads

Trim both ends to the desired length. Insert the metal beads and close with overhand knots. Finished.

44. Creeper Knot

The creeper knot is a basic knot with a very long history. It is often used in ring and chain forms. The 3 outer loops of the creeper knot can be set into articles for decoration.

Knot Type
Basic single knot

Suggested Materials
1 cord: 2.5 mm (Dia.), 30 cm (L)

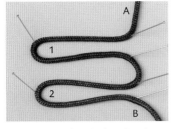

1 Pin the cord on the board as shown with 2 loops. The top loop is 1 and the bottom is 2. The top cord end is A and the bottom is B.

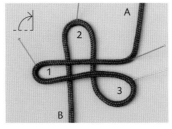

2 Turn loop 2 clockwise under loop 1. Loop 3 is formed on the lower right. Set with pins.

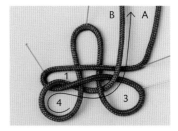

3 Take cord B to the left and turn clockwise. Pass it through loop 1 from the front and pass through loop 3 from the back. Take end B to the upper right. Loop 4 is formed.

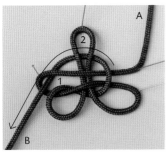

4 Move cord B to the left under loop 2. Then turn it to the lower left, passing through loop 1 from the back. The base is set.

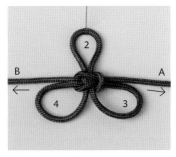

5 Pull gently both ends outwards to tighten the knot. Note that the 3 loops are to be identical in size.

6 Adjust the shape and make sure the knot is secure. Done!

Earring
Cord: 1 dark green cord, 2.5 mm (Dia.), 30 cm (L)
Findings: 1 cord end cap, 1 earring hook
Accessory: 1 light green jade bead with 1 jump ring

1 First is to make a creeper knot. Then move the cord ends up and set them next to the 2 top loops. Trim and seal the ends together to form a teardrop shape.

2 Tuck the cord ends into the cord end cap with the earring hook. Attach the light green jade bead to the bottom loop.

45. Sauvastika Creeper Knot

The sauvastika creeper knot is a tiny knot derived from the creeper knot. The difference between the two knots is the center portion. The middle of the creeper knot is a flat knot, whereas that of the sauvastika creeper knot is a sauvastika knot.

Knot Type
Innovative decorative knot

Suggested Materials
1 cord: 2.5 mm (Dia.), 40 cm (L)

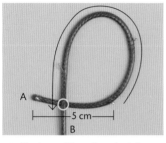

1 Pin the cord 5 cm from the left. The left side is A and the right side is B. The following steps are focused on twining cord B. First, take cord B up and anticlockwise over cord A to form a loop.

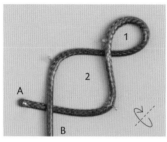

2 Hold the tip of the loop and twist upwards to create another loop. The top loop is 1 and the other loop is 2.

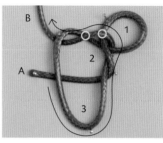

3 Insert cord B into loop 2 from the front and pull it out from loop 1. Take cord B over and under the top of loop 2 and pull it out from the left. Pull cord end B upwards to form loop 3 under loop 2 as shown.

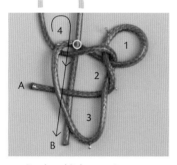

4 Bend cord B down, going over-under-under-under the left side of loops 2 & 3 to form loop 4.

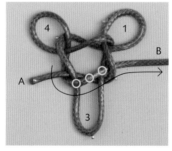

5 As shown in the figure, loop 4 is identical to loop 1. Take cord B to the right, going over-over-over-under the loops. The base is set.

6 Tighten the knot by pulling both ends and loops 1, 3 & 4. A sauvastika knot is formed in the center. Adjust the loops so that it is symmetrical.

Necklace
Cord: 1 blue waxed cord, 2.5 mm (Dia.), 100 cm (L)
Finding: 1 jump ring
Accessory: 1 blue fish glass bead

1 First is to make a sauvastika creeper knot. Attach the jump ring with the blue fish glass bead to the bottom loop.

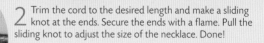

2 Trim the cord to the desired length and make a sliding knot at the ends. Secure the ends with a flame. Pull the sliding knot to adjust the size of the necklace. Done!

46. Tassel Knot

The tassel knot is a basic knot with a very long history. Being popular in the Tang dynasty, it was introduced to Japan and eventually widespread. It has a cross pattern in the middle, meaning longevity and auspiciousness. Its classic and attractive outlook makes a good gift wrapping element.

Knot Type
Basic single knot

Suggested Materials
1 cord: 2.5 mm (Dia.), 120 cm (L)

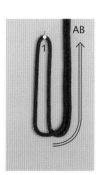 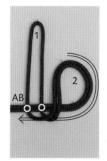 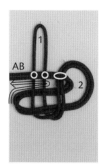  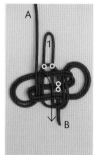

1 Pin at the center of the cord. The left side is A and the right is B. Bring cords A & B together and move them to the right and then up. Set with pins. Loop 1 is formed on the left.

2 Turn cords A & B to the right and clockwise, going under the upper part of the cords and over loop 1. Loop 2 is formed on the right.

3 Pass cords A & B back to the right and under loop 1. Then pull them out from loop 2. Take cords A & B back to the left, going over the left side of loop 2 and then loop1.

4 Take cords A & B down and anticlockwise, going under-over-over the cords to form loop 3.

5 Now let's separate the cords. Take cord B to the right over loop 1. Then move it down, going under-over-under-under the double cords.

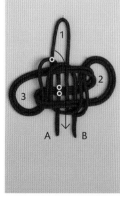   

6 Take cord A to the right over the right side of loop 1. Then move it down, going under-over the double cords, then under the cords. The base is set.

7 Gently tighten the knot by pulling both ends and loops 1, 2 & 3. Adjust loops and be sure the knot is symmetrical.

8 The size of the loops can be modified per your design. The tassel knot is done. The left figure is the front and the right figure is the back. Apply the tassel knot onto a fabric pouch. It is not only a fastener but also a decorative element.

47. Two-Outer-Loop Cloverleaf Knot

The two-outer-loop cloverleaf knot is a symbol of luck. It has a wide range of applications and can be combined with other knots to create various types of accessories and ornaments.

Knot Type
Basic single knot

Suggested Materials
1 cord: 2.5 mm (Dia.), 50 cm (L)

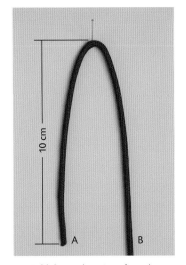

1 Fold the cord at 10 cm from the left. Set with a pin. The left side is A and the right is B.

2 Make a U-bend with cord B and turn it to the left, going over cord B and under cord A. Set with a pin.

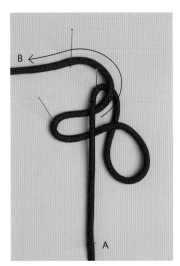

3 Take end B upwards and set with a pin.

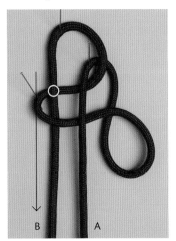

4 Bend cord B downwards, going over and under the left loop.

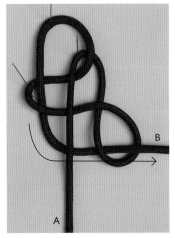

5 Turn cord B to the right, as shown in the figure, passing under cord A, and going under the left side of the right loop.

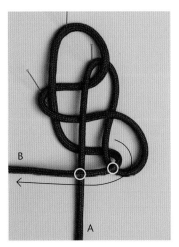

6 Turn cord B to the left over the cord.

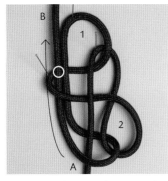 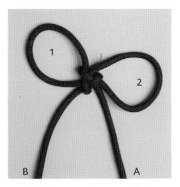 

7 Bring cord B upwards, going under and over the loop. Identify the 2 outer loops before final shaping.

8 Pull the 2 outer loops and the 2 ends at the same time to tighten the knot.

9 Adjust the size of the loops as shown. Done!

Butterfly Ornament
Cord: 2 red cords, 2.5 mm (Dia.), 70 cm (L)
Accessories: 2 beads

1 Create 2 symmetrical two-outer-loop cloverleaf knots on the same cord. Make sure the space in between is appropriate to represent the abdomen of the butterfly.

2 Form a double-connection knot with the 2 ends. Trim the ends to the desired length as the butterfly antennas.

3 Insert 2 beads, one at each end. Scure the end with a flame. Use a pair of pliers to pinch the middle of the cord between the 2 knots to form a crease, which represents the abdomen.

Fig. 53 The cloverleaf knot can be modified to different knot types. Top left: butterfly ornament composed of 2 two-outer-loop cloverleaf knots and double-connection knot. Top right: green cloverleaf knot earring. Bottom left & middle: brown and red brooches composed of four cloverleaf knots. Bottom right: vertical cloverleaf knot barrette.

48. Cloverleaf Knot

The name of the cloverleaf knot is simply derived from its shape. It is a symbol of luck. The knot can be tweaked to form other modified knots and often used to make pendants and ornaments. The application is flexible.

Knot Type
Basic single knot

Suggested Materials
1 cord: 2.5 mm (Dia.), 60 cm (L)

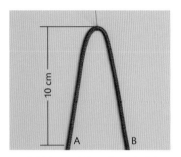

1 Fold the cord 10 cm from the left. Set with a pin. The left side is A and the right is B.

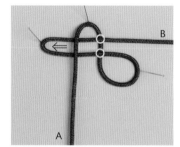

2 As shown in the figure, form a U-bend with cord B, turn it to the left, going over cord B and under cord A.

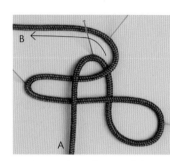

3 Bring end B to the upper left. Set with a pin.

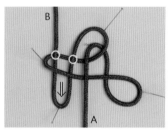

4 Form a U-bend with cord B. Turn it downwards, passing over and under the left loop. Set with a pin.

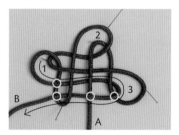

5 Turn cord B to the lower left, going over and under the loop that is just created. Place it under cord A. Then pass it under and over the right loop. Bring it down and to the left, going over-over-under-over the cord. The base is done.

6 Before shaping, identify the 3 outer loops. Pull the both ends and the 3 outer loops to tighten the knot. Adjust the size of the outer loops. The cloverleaf is complete.

Earring
Cord: 1 green cord, 2 mm (Dia.), 60 cm (L)
Finding: 1 earing hook

2 Reserve enough cord ends to form a outer loop and trim the excess. Connect the 2 ends with a flame.

1 First is to make a cloverleaf knot. Then insert the earring hook into one of the ends.

3 Conceal the joint by moving it inside the center of the knot. Adjust the shape. The earring is finished.

49. Vertical Cloverleaf Knot

The vertical cloverleaf knot is very common in Chinese knotting with a lot of variations. It has a wide range of applications, such as pendants and accessories.

Knot Type
Basic single knot

Suggested Materials
1 cord: 4 mm (W), 60 cm (L)

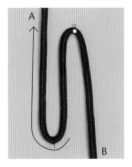

1 Pin the middle of the cord on the board. The left side is A and the right is B. Bend cord A upwards to form a U-bend.

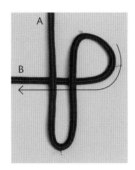

2 Turn cord B to the left and under the U-bend. Set with pins.

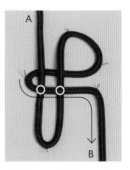

3 Turn cord B down and to the right, passing over the U-bend. Set with a pin. Bring cord B downwards.

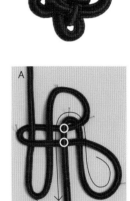

4 Turn cord B clockwise and up, passing under the U-bend. Bring cord B down and over the U-bend.

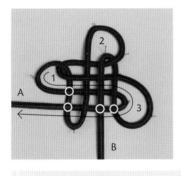

5 Turn cord A anticlockwise to form a loop. Move it to the right, going over and under the first U-bend, then under the right U-bend. Turn cord A to the left, going over the first U-bend, then under and over the left U-bend. The base is done.

6 Before shaping, identify the 3 outer loops. Tighten the knot and adjust the outer loops so that they are identical. The knot is finished.

Barrette
Cord: 1 red flat cord, 4 mm (W), 80 cm (L)
Finding: 1 metal barrette

1 First is to make vertical cloverleaf knots until it reaches the desire length. Reserve enough cord ends to form an outer loop and trim.

2 Seal the ends with a flame. Conceal the joint by moving it inside the knot. This is the back of the accessory.

3 Choose a proper size metal barrette. Use hot glue to attach the barrette to the knot. The barrette is complete!

50. *Ruyi* Knot

The *ruyi* knot is a combination of various cloverleaf knots. It has a wide range of applications as well as auspicious meaning: "blessings in four seasons," "as you wish," and "harmony."

Knot Type
Modified single knot

Suggested Materials
1 cord: 4 mm (W), 120 cm (L)

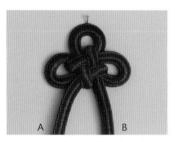

1 Create a cloverleaf knot by referring to the instructions of the horizontal cloverleaf knot. The left side is A and the right side is B.

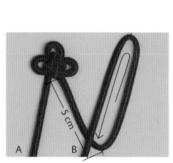

2 Next is to create a horizontal cloverleaf knot with cord B on the right. Pin cord B 5 cm away from the cloverleaf knot. Turn cord B to the upper right and anticlockwise to form a long loop. Set with pins.

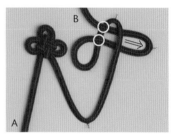

3 Form a U-bend with cord B, shift it to the right and tuck it into the long loop. Set with pins. A horizontal loop is formed on the right.

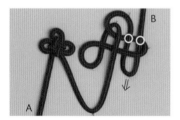

4 Form another U-bend and shift it downwards, going over and under the horizontal loop.

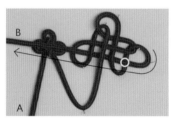

5 Turn cord B to the left, going over-under-under-under the loops.

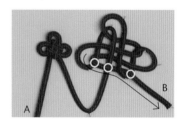

6 Bend cord B to the right, going over-over-under-over the loops. The base of the cloverleaf knot on the right is set.

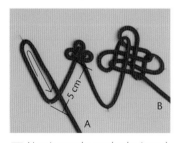

7 Next is to make another horizontal cloverleaf knot on the left. Pin cord A 5 cm from the center cloverleaf knot, take it to the upper left and turn it clockwise to form a long loop.

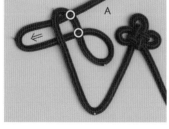

8 Make a U-bend and shift it to the left, going over and under the long loop to form a horizontal loop on the left. Set with pins.

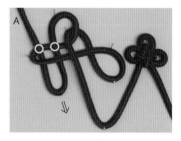

9 Create another U-bend and tuck it downwards, going over and under the horizontal loop.

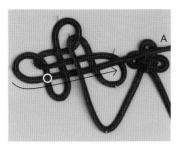

10 Turn cord A downwards and anticlockwise, going over-under-under-under the loops.

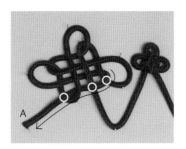

11 Take cord A to the left, going over-over-under-over the loops. The base of the cloverleaf knot on the left is set.

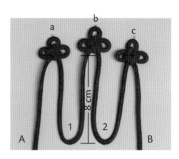

12 Tighten the 2 cloverleaf knots on the outside so that they match the one in the middle. Let's name the cloverleaf knots from left to right a, b & c. The loops in between are loops 1 & 2. They are about 8 cm in length.

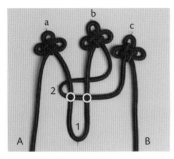

13 Shift loop 2 to the upper left and tuck loop 1 into loop 2.

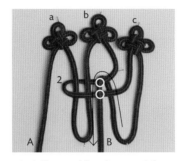

14 Turn cord B to the upper left under loop 2. Take cord B downwards over loop 2.

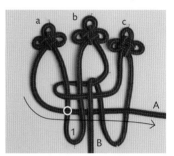

15 Bend cord A to the right, going over-under-under-under the loops.

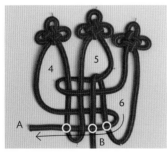

16 Move cord A to the left, going over-over-under-over the loops. The base of the 4th cloverleaf knot is set. The 3 loops of the 4th cloverleaf knot are indicated on the figure.

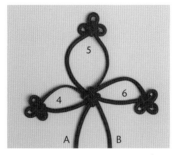

17 Identify the 3 loops of the 4th cloverleaf knot and tight the knot. It is just like a big cloverleaf knot with small cloverleaf knots at the tips of the loops.

18 Further tighten the 4th cloverleaf knot by shifting the cord towards the ends. The ruyi knot, which combines a left, right and center knots, is complete.

Brooch

Cord: 1 red flat cord, 4 mm (W), 120 cm (L)

Finding: 1 bar pin

1 First is to make a *ruyi* knot. Then create a vertical cloverleaf knot at the bottom. Tighten it so that it links to the *ruyi* knot. *Ruyi*-harmony knot is created. Trim the cord ends to enclose the bottom loop.

2 Connect the ends with a flame and conceal the joint by shifting it to the knot.

3 Choose a proper size bar pin. Attach the bar pin to the knot by using hot glue. Flip it over and the *ruyi*-harmony knot brooch is complete.

51. Papaya Knot

The papaya knot looks like 4 papayas being tied up together; hence the name. It has a meaning of fruitful and successful, which is good for decoration on accessories and gifts.
When making the papaya knot, the size of the loops is to be the same as the finished product. Be sure they are neat and identical to achieve the best result.

Knot Type
Modified single knot

Suggested Materials
1 cord: 2.5 mm (Dia.), 60 cm (L)

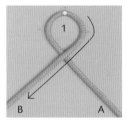

1 Pin the middle of the cord. The left side is A and the right is B. As shown, cross cord B over cord A to form loop 1.

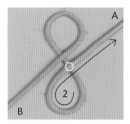

2 Take cord A to the left and turn clockwise over the upper part of cord A to form loop 2.

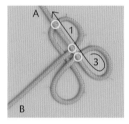

3 Take cord A down and turn clockwise over the upper part of cord A and loop 1. Bring it to the upper left. Loop 3 is formed.

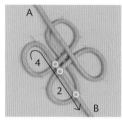

4 Take cord B to the upper right and turn it clockwise to the lower right, going over the upper part of cord B and loop 2. Loop 4 is formed.

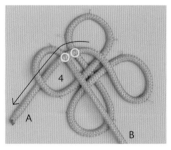

5 As shown in the figure, pass cord A from the upper right through loop 4 from the front.

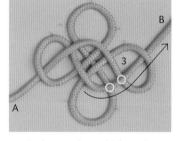

6 As shown, take cord B from the lower right to pass through loop 3 from the front.

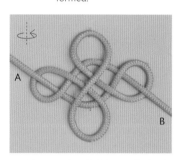

7 Flip over the whole knot. The back is now the front. Set with pins.

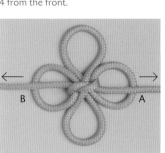

8 Make an overhand knot in the middle with both ends. The base is set. Pull both ends to shape as shown.

9 Flip over the knot. The back now is the front. Adjust the shape to complete the papaya knot. Place the papaya knot onto the desired area as decoration. Adjust the size of the loops in proportion to the wallet.

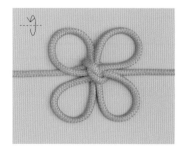

52. Chinese Lute Knot

This knot is named due to the shape that resembles the traditional Chinese instrument called lute or pipa. It is often combined with a button knot as a functional and decorative element on clothing. Other popular applications are earrings, hair accessories, and brooches.

Knot Type
Modified single knot

Suggested Materials
1 cord: 2.5 mm (Dia.), 60 cm (L)

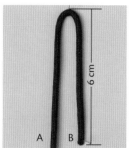 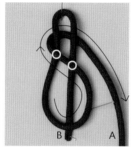

1 Pin the cord 6 cm from the right. The left side is A and the right is B. We will mainly work on cord A. Bend cord A anticlockwise over the cord to form a loop. Then wrap it backwards under the cord.

 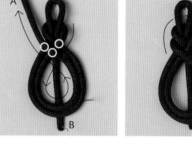

2 As shown, take cord A to the lower left, going anticlockwise around the internal side of the first loop, taking end A to the upper left. Take cord A to the right under the U-bend and below the upper wrap.

3 Repeat step 2 to create two more loops as shown.

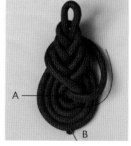 

4 Bring end A down and pass it through the middle hole from the front. The base is done. Pull cord A and adjust the shape.

5 Turn over the knot and trim the ends.

6 Seal the ends to the back of the knot with a flame. Done. The left is the back and the right is the front. For durability, thread the back of the knot to secure the shape.

53. Button Knot

The button knot is one of the most widely spread basic knots. It has been used as buttons for a long time; hence the name. The knot shape is like a diamond, which makes it very decorative beside its practical value. Sometimes, it is arranged in a series as necklaces and bracelets.

Knot Type
Basic single knot

Suggested Materials
1 cord: 2.5 mm (Dia.), 50 cm (L)

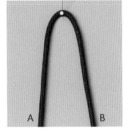

1 Fold the cord in half and pin the middle. The left side is A and the right is B.

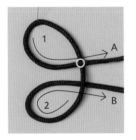

2 Take cord A to the right over cord B to form a loop. Take cord B to the left, turning clockwise to form another loop under the cord.

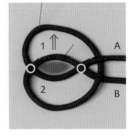

3 As shown, move loop 2 up, partially overlapping loop 1 to create a lens shape. Set with pins.

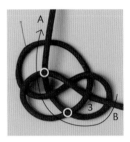

4 Now we will work on cord A. Move it down and under cord B. Turn clockwise, going over and under the loops. Then pull it out from the lens opening.

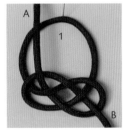

5 Arrange the knot as shown in the figure. Pull to enlarge loop 1 and create a diamond hole at the intersection of the loops.

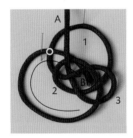

6 Take cord B clockwise, going over the left side of loop 1 and under loops 2 & 3. Then pull it out from the diamond hole.

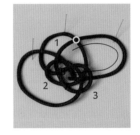

7 Turn cord A clockwise over the right side of loop 1 and under loops 2 & 3. Pull it out from the diamond hole.

8 Pull out and parallel both ends. The base is set.

9 Next is shaping. Hold the ends and pull the knot upwards. Reduce the size of the knot by stretching the ends downwards. Further tighten the knot by pulling the ends and loop together. Do not pull too hard. Make sure the knot is even and round. Note that the knot is in the middle.

Porcelain Bead Necklace
Cords: 2 pink cords, 2.5 mm (Dia.), 130 cm (L)
Findings: 1 pair of necklace clasps, 2 ribbon clamps
Accessories: 5 porcelain beads (1 bigger & 4 smaller), 10 metal spacer beads

2 Create some button knots next to the last beads, 4 on each side. Insert a metal spacer bead between the knots. Finish the cord ends by making them into two-strand braids.

1 Choose 1 big porcelain beads and 4 same size smaller beads. Make 2 button knots between the beads. Add a small metal spacer bead between the knots for decoration.

3 Attach a pair of ribbon clamps to the ends. Fasten with a pair of necklace clasps. Finished.

Modified Button Knot and Chinese Lute Knot Button
Cords: 2 red cords, 2.5 mm (Dia.), 90 cm (L)

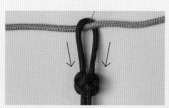

1 Choose a supplementary cord that is the same diameter of the button knot cord. Pass it through the top loop. To compress the top loop, identify its path and end. Pull the relevant end, and the top loop will be reduced. Meanwhile, a new loop will be protruded from the knot. Repeat the same step to tighten the new loop.

The original location of the supplementary cord

2 Continue with the same step until all loops are closed. Pull to tighten the knot and remove the supplementary cord. Adjust the shape. The knot is now on top with 2 ends below and no loose loop on top. Form a Chinese lut knot with the loose ends. One side of the button is done.

3 Then create another Chinese lute knot. Push the loop into the modified button knot. A set of Chinese lute knot button is finished.

54. Simple Button Knot

The simple button knot is a popular decorative knot. It is very strong and not easy to be deformed. To apply on necklaces, bracelets and belts, it can be arranged in a series with other decorative elements.

The simple button knot is a variation of the button knot. It has the cord ends on both sides of the knot. The knot is usually in the middle of the cord.

Knot Type
Modified single knot

Suggested Materials
1 cord: 2.5 mm (Dia.), 50 cm (L)

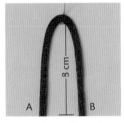

1 Pin the cord 8 cm from the right. The left side is A and the right is B. We only twine with cord A.

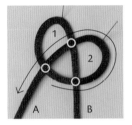

2 Take cord A to the right and turn anticlockwise over the cord. As shown in the figure, 2 loops are formed with one on top of the other.

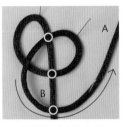

3 Take cord A to the upper left and over cord B.

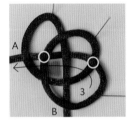

4 Then turn it back to the left, going over-under-over-under the loops. The third loop is formed, creating a diamond opening in the middle.

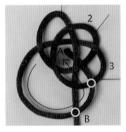

5 Bring cord A to the lower right, going anticlockwise over cord B, passing over-under-under the loops.

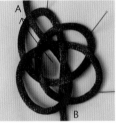

6 Pull cord A out from the diamond opening. The base is done.

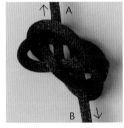

7 Next is shaping. Pull both ends gently to tighten the knot.

8 Adjust to finish the simple button knot.

Porcelain Tube Bracelet
Cord: 1 red cord, 2.5 mm (Dia.), 80 cm (L)
Accessory: 1 porcelain tube bead

1 Insert the porcelain tube bead into the cord. Create 2 simple button knots, one at each end.

2 Trim the ends to the desired length. Tie the ends with a sliding knot.

3 Finished.

55. Double Button Knot

This is also a variation of the button knot. The knot is firm and relatively bigger, and commonly used as pendent accessories of keys and thumb drives. It can also be combined with other knots to create different types of ornaments.

Knot Type
Modified single knot

Suggested Materials
1 cord: 2.5 mm (Dia.), 80 cm (L)

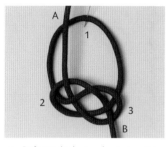

1 Refer to the button knot steps 1 to 5 to arrange the cord as shown in the figure. The top part of the cord is A and the bottom is B. Note that we have 3 loops here.

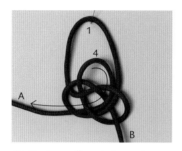

2 Next, we will create 2 more loops. Bend cord A clockwise, going around the internal side of the loop 1, passing it out from loop 3. The 4th loop is formed.

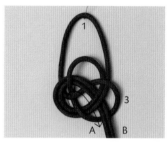

3 Keep following the path of loop 1, pull end A out from loop 3, setting it parallel to cord B.

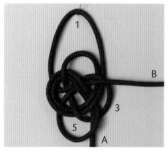

4 Let's work on cord B. Turn it clockwise to form a loop over cord A and under the left side of loop 1. Move cord B along the internal side of loop 3. This is loop 5. Note that a diamond opening is formed in the middle.

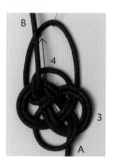

5 Continue to move cord B along loops 3 and 4.

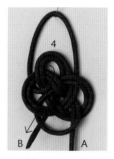

6 After curling along the internal side of loop 4, pull cord B out from the diamond hole in the center.

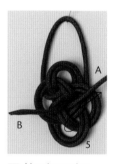

7 Next is to twine cord A. Take cord A along the internal side of loop 5 and pull it out from the diamond hole. The base is done.

8 Next is shaping. Pull out both ends at the same time. Remove all pins and push the knot upwards.

9 Pull the loop and both ends gently. Tighten the knot by stretching the cord towards the ends. Adjust accordingly. Done! Trim the ends below the knot. Seal the ends with a flame and tuck them inside the knot. Attach to a key using a binding knot.

56. Button Ring Knot

As the name implies, the button ring knot is in a form of a ring. The construction is based on the button knot that is shaped around a cylinder. The knot is comparatively firm; therefore it can be used as a napkin holder or decorative pencil topper.

Knot Type
Modified single knot

Suggested Materials
1 cord: 2.5 mm (Dia.), 120 cm (L)

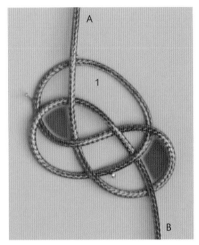

1 Follow the button knot steps 1 to 4 to twine the knot as shown in the figure. The top is cord A and the bottom is cord B. Note the shaded areas.

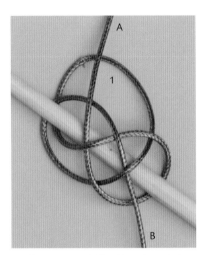

2 Pass a pen or similar object through the shaded areas.

3 Enlarge loop 1 as shown.

4 Pass cord A through loop 1 from the front. Adjust the shape accordingly. Now cord A is at the back and cord B is in the front.

 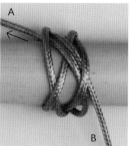 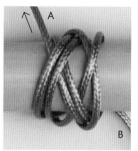 

5 Loop cord A to the front and follow the path of cord B. Keep turning the pen and take the cord in and out along the path until the knot is doubled. Stop the interlacing. Pull cord A out. Now let's work on cord B, which is similar.

6 Take cord B to the lower left from the back. Following the same path, interlace the cord along the internal side of the double cord. Keep turning the pen and pass the cord in and out until the knot is tripled. Stop the interlacing. Pull cord B out. The base is set.

7 Remove the pen and gently tighten the knot.

8 Trim and seal the ends with a flame. Shift the cord to conceal the joint. The button ring knot is complete. The key technique is to make sure both ends follow the primary path side by side in sequence to triple the knot.

9 The two figures present the different views. Insert the button ring knot into a pen or brush for decoration.

57. Auspicious Cloud Knot

The shape of the auspicious cloud knot is similar to the Chinese cloud pattern; hence the name. Traditionally, Chinese believe that clouds deliver rains, which water and moisturize all things. They also believe that clouds are the homes and conveyances of the gods. "Cloud" (*yun*, 云) is a homophone of "luck" (*yun*, 运), which makes it a symbol of blessing.

The application of the auspicious cloud knot is very broad since the configuration is very neat and beautiful. It is commonly used in necklaces, bracelets and belts.

Its fabrication is similar to the button knot except the final process—shaping—which leads to a different pattern.

Knot Type
Modified single knot

Suggested Materials
1 cord: 2.5 mm (Dia.),
    50 cm (L)

1 Follow the button knot instructions until you reach the configuration as shown in the figure.

Small loop

2 Next is shaping. Push the knot upwards, leaving a small loop on top. Make sure the knot is not too tight for the next step.

3 As shown, press the top loop down and through the knot.

4 Pull both ends to tighten the knot.

5 Adjust the shape as shown. The left figure is the front and the right is the back. They are not identical.

Ring
Cord: 1 red cord,
    2.5 mm (Dia.),
    50 cm (L)
Tools: 1 braided
    silk cord,
    double-sided
    tape

1 First is to make an auspicious cloud knot. Trim the ends to the desired ring size. Seal the ends with a flame.

2 Coil double-sided tape around the joint.

3 Coil a braided silk cord around the double-sided tape and secure with a flame. The ring is done.

58. Heart Knot

The heart shape spontaneously directs you to think about love. The heart knot, therefore, is the most popular knot to be applied on ornaments, e.g. bracelets, to express love.

Knot Type
Modified single knot

Suggested Materials
1 cord: 2.5 mm (Dia.), 50 cm (L)

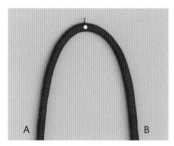

1 Pin the cord in the middle. The left side is A and the right is B.

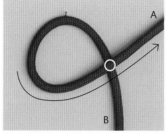

2 Take cord A to the upper right over cord B to form a loop.

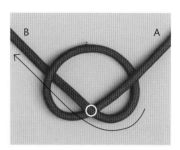

3 Move cord B to the upper left, going through the loop from the front.

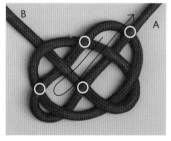

4 Bend cord A anticlockwise to the lower left, going over-under-over the loop. Then take it back to the upper right, going under-over-under-over the loops. The base is set.

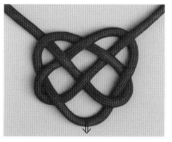

5 Get ready for shaping. Pull the bottom center of the loop downwards as shown. Be sure the overall shape is symmetrical.

6 Pull gently to tighten the knot.

Necklace
Cord: 1 red flat cord, 4 mm (W), 90 cm (L)
Finding: 1 jump ring
Accessory: 1 red butterfly glass bead

1 First is to make a heart knot. Attach the jump ring and the red butterfly glass bead at the bottom of the knot.

2 Trim the cord ends to the desired length and create a sliding knot.

3 The necklace is done.

59. Five-Loop Ten-Hole Cage Knot

The cage knot is similar to the mesh pattern on the Chinese bamboo cage; hence the name. It is often used to exorcise evils. The five-loop ten-hole cage knot is commonly applied for decoration. Examples are brooches, hair barrettes, ornaments, and coasters.

Knot Type
Modified single knot

Suggested Materials
1 cord: 2.5 mm (Dia.), 50 cm (L)

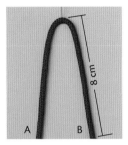

1 Pin the cord 8 cm from the right. The left side is cord A, the active cord, and the right is B.

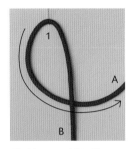

2 Move cord A to the right under cord B. This is loop 1.

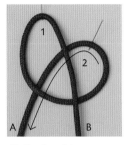

3 Bend cord A anticlockwise under loop 1. Loop 2 is formed.

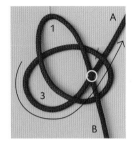

4 Move cord A to the upper right, going under loop 1 and over cord A to form loop 3.

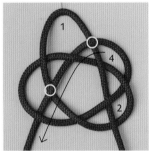

5 Turn cord A back to the lower left, going over-under-over-under the loops as shown. Loop 4 is formed between loops 1 & 2 at the upper right. The base is set.

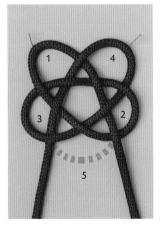

6 The next step is shaping. Adjust according to the figure to ensure the knot is symmetrical and the loops are identical. After trimming and enclosing the ends, the 5th loop will be formed. The knot is done. There is a pentagon in the middle. There are altogether 5 small and 5 big holes. Thus, it is named 10-hole cage knot.

Plum Blossom Decoration
Cord: 1 red cord, 2.5 mm (Dia.), 100 cm (L)

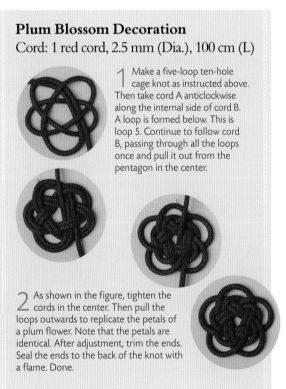

1 Make a five-loop ten-hole cage knot as instructed above. Then take cord A anticlockwise along the internal side of cord B. A loop is formed below. This is loop 5. Continue to follow cord B, passing through all the loops once and pull it out from the pentagon in the center.

2 As shown in the figure, tighten the cords in the center. Then pull the loops outwards to replicate the petals of a plum flower. Note that the petals are identical. After adjustment, trim the ends. Seal the ends to the back of the knot with a flame. Done.

60. Five-Loop Fifteen-Hole Cage Knot

After making the five-loop ten-hole cage knot, let's learn how to make a five-loop fifteen-hole cage knot.

Knot Type
Modified single knot

Suggested Materials
1 cord: 2.5 mm (Dia.), 80 cm (L)

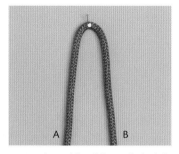

1 Pin the middle of the cord. The left side is A and the right is B.

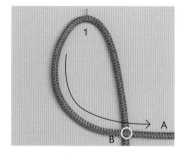

2 Turn cord A to the right over cord B to form loop 1.

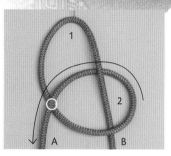

3 Bend cord A anticlockwise, going under and over loop 1. This is loop 2.

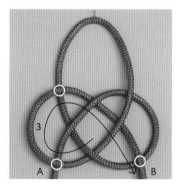

4 Move cord B to the left over cord A. Turn it clockwise, going over-under-under-over the loops. Loop 3 is formed.

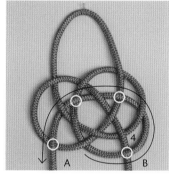

5 Take cord A to the right over cord B, going anticlockwise under-over-under-over the loops. Loop 4 is formed. The base is set.

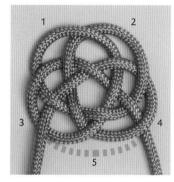

6 Adjust the knot so that the loops are identical with proper spacing. Trim the ends and seal them together with a flame to form loop 5 below. There is a pentagon in the middle. There are altogether 15 holes.

Placemat Decoration
Cord: 1 yellow cord,
2.5 mm (Dia.),
80 cm (L)

1 First is to make the five-loop fifteen-hole cage knot. Trim the ends to form a loop and seal them with a flame.

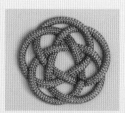

2 Shift the joint over an intersection. The left figure is the back and the right is the front. Flip over the cage knot and attach it to a placemat.

61. Five-Loop Pineapple Knot

This knot is created by combining the techniques of the five-loop fifteen-hole cage knot and the pineapple knot. This strong knot is based on the five loops of the fifteen-hole cage knot and the interlacing technique of the pineapple knot.

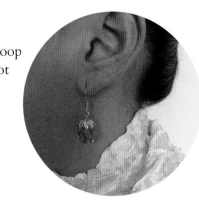

Knot Type
Modified single knot

Suggested Materials
1 cord: 2.5 mm (Dia.), 100 cm (L)

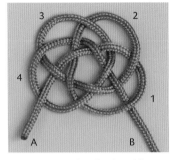

1 First is to make a five-loop fifteen-hole cage knot. Let's identify the 4 outside loops, cord A and cord B.

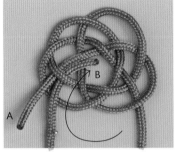

2 Next is to double the knot by running cord B along the internal side of the loops. Take cord B to the upper left, turn clockwise, and go along the internal side of loop 1. Loop 5 is formed below. Adjust it to match the other loops.

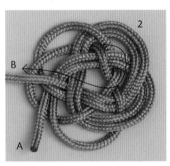

3 Continue to move cord B clockwise along the internal side of loop 2.

4 Continue to follow the path along the internal side of loop 3.

5 Keep moving cord B clockwise along the internal side of loop 4.

6 Last round, take cord B clockwise along the internal side of loop 5 and pull it out from point C. The base is set.

7 Next is shaping. Pull cord B so that the center of the knot gets higher to form a hemisphere. The left figure is the top view and the right figure is the side view.

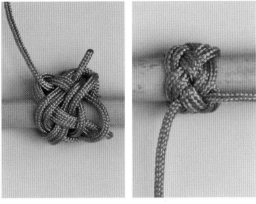

8 Push a pen or similar object into the center of the knot. Then pull the cord up and down to tighten the knot.

9 Pull out the pen. The figures above present the different views.

10 Tuck the ends into the gaps and pull them out from the other side.

11 Trim and seal the ends with a flame so that they stay inside the knot. The five-loop pineapple knot is complete. The left figure is the side view and the right figure is the top view.

Earring

Cord: 1 gold cord, 2 mm (Dia.), 100 cm (L)

Findings: 2 gold floral bead caps, 1 head pin, 1 earring hook

1 Push the metal head pin through the floral bead cap.

2 Then insert a five-loop pineapple knot to the pin. Insert the other floral bead cap to wrap around the knot.

3 Bend the end of the head pin to form 2 small loops to prevent the bead cap from sliding out.

4 Attach the earring hook to the loop. The earring is done.

62. Six-Loop Cage Knot

We have introduced the five-loop ten-hole cage knot and five-loop fifteen-hole cage knot in the earlier sections. Now we will learn how to make a cage knot with 6 loops around.

Knot Type
Modified single knot

Suggested Materials
1 cord: 3.5 mm (Dia.), 80 cm (L)

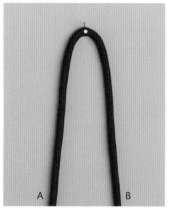

1 Pin the middle of the cord. The left side is A and the right is B.

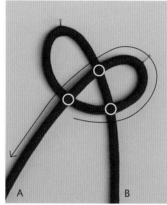

2 Take cord A to the upper right and turn anticlockwise to form a loop over cord B.

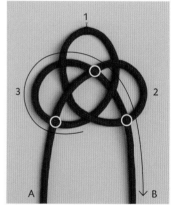

3 Take cord B to the left over cord A and turn it clockwise, going under-over-under-over the loops. Let both cord ends down. Three loops are formed interlocking each other.

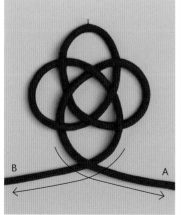

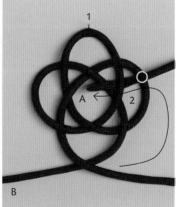

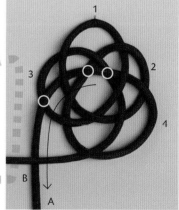

4 In this step, we will create the 4th loop. Bend both ends towards the middle, where cord A overlaps cord B. Turn cord A anticlockwise, going over and under loops 1 & 2, then going over-over-under-over the other loops. Move cord end A under end B.

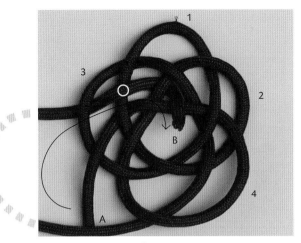

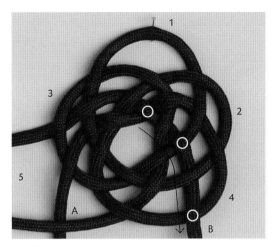

5 Next is to form the 5ᵗʰ loop. Take cord B clockwise, going under-over-under the loops. Let's stop here and identify the pentagon in the middle.

6 We will change the pentagon into a hexagon. Take cord B over-under-over to pass through the upper right corner of the pentagon from the back. Then move it under-over the loops.

7 Loop 5 is formed at the lower left. The base is set.

8 Adjust the shape so that it is symmetrical with proper spacing. Done! Trim the ends, reserving enough cord length to form a loop. Seal them together with a flame. Shift the cord to conceal the join. The decoration is done.

Fig. 54 The cage knot can be modified to different knot types. Front row, from left to right: octagonal cage knot, five-loop ten-hole cage knot, six-loop cage knot ornaments. On bamboo mat: heart knot necklace with red butterfly glass pendant.

63. Octagonal Cage Knot

The octagonal cage knot belongs to the cage knot family. The round shape makes it good for coasters, brooches, and other decorative elements.

Knot Type
Modified single knot

Suggested Materials
1 cord: 3.5 mm (W), 60 cm (L)

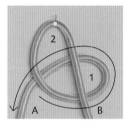

1 Pin the center of the cord. The left side is A and the right side is B. Turn cord A anticlockwise to the right to form loop 1. Shift loop 1 to the right under cord B to form loop 2.

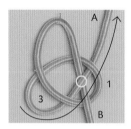

2 Move cord A to the upper right, going under-over-under loop 1. Loop 3 is formed.

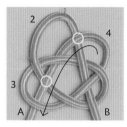

3 Take cord A to the lower left, going over-under-over-under the loops. Loop 4 is formed.

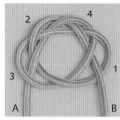

4 Pull both cord ends downwards to tighten the 4 loops as shown in the figure.

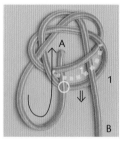

5 Enlarge loop 1. Bring cord A upwards, going over and under loop 1.

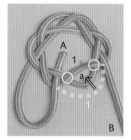

6 Shift the lower part of loop 1 upwards and over the adjacent loop to create hole a. Set with pins.

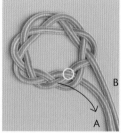

7 Take cord A to the right, going over and under hole A. Pull out cord A and the base is set.

8 Pull both ends and adjust the holes so that they are identical. The knot is complete.

Cellphone Charm
Cord: 1 yellow flat cord, 3.5 mm (W), 60 cm (L)
Finding: 1 cellphone strap
Accessory: 1 lucky cat charm with a small bell

1 First is to make an octagonal cage knot. Trim the cord ends to form the last loop. Enclose the ends with a flame. Shift the joint over another cord to conceal.

2 Flip the knot over. This is the front side of the knot. Attach the lucky cat charm and the octagonal cage knot to the cellphone strap.

64. Masthead Knot

In Chinese, the masthead knot is called *hua man jie*, which is a popular Buddhist auspicious symbol of relieving all out of the sinful world. This knot can be used as ornaments, pendants, and gift decorations.

Knot Type
Modified single knot

Suggested Materials
1 cord: 3 mm (Dia.), 80 cm (L)

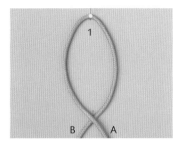

1 Pin the cord in the middle. The left side is A and the right is B. As shown, make loop 1 where the intersection is in the middle and cord A is over cord B.

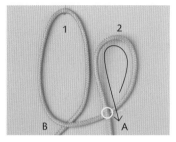

2 Bend cord A up, going anticlockwise over the upper part of cord A. This is loop 2. Set with pins.

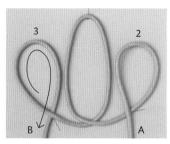

3 Take cord B up, going clockwise and under the upper part of cord B. This is loop 3. Note that the size of loop 3 is the same as loop 2.

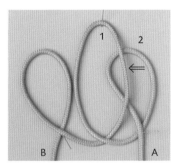

4 Move loop 2 slightly to the left and under the right side of loop 1.

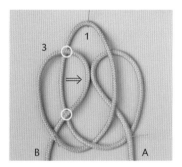

5 Move loop 3 slightly to the right and over the left side of loop 1.

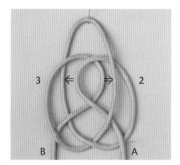

6 As shown, move the left side of loop 2 to the left. Move the right side of loop 3 to the right.

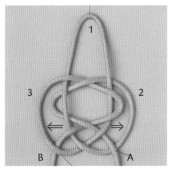

7 Pull the left side of loop 2 out between loops 1 & 3. Pull the right side of loop 3 out between loops 1 & 2.

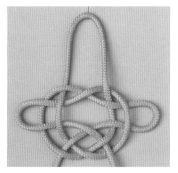

8 The base is set. Adjust the knot so that it is symmetrical with proper spacing.

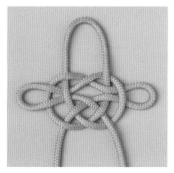

9 Done! Tying a scroll/gift with the masthead knot presents both practical and aesthetic quality.

65. Interaction Knot

The Five Elements is the classical Taoist philosophy emphasizing the interaction of both generating and restraining among wood, fire, earth, metal, and water. The interaction knot represents harmony and is commonly applied on ornaments for festivals and temples. It can also be part of clothing, hair accessories, gifts, pillar and home decorations.

Knot Type
Modified single knot

Suggested Materials
1 cord: 3 mm (Dia.), 60 cm (L)

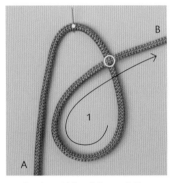

1 Pin the middle of the cord. The left side is A and the right is B. Take cord B to the upper right, turning clockwise to form a loop over the upper part of cord B. This is loop 1.

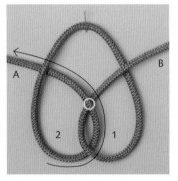

2 Turn cord A anticlockwise, passing it through loop 1 from the back and under the upper part of cord A. This is loop 2. Now loops 1 & 2 are interlocking.

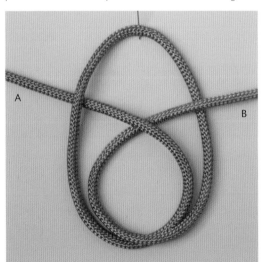

3 Stretch the interlocking area in the middle as shown.

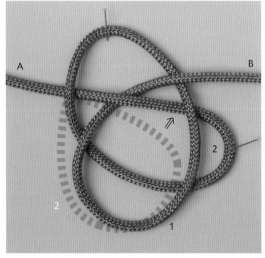

4 Pull loop 2 to the right under loop 1.

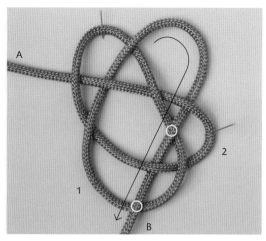

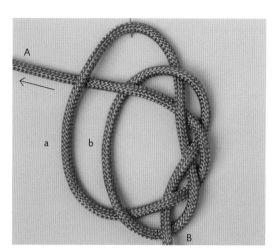

5 Bring cord B downwards, going under-over-under-over the loops.

6 Pull cord A towards the left and adjust the shape as shown in the diagram. The interlacement on the right is close together while 2 arcs are formed on the left. The leftmost arc is a and the other is b.

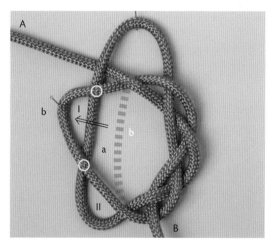

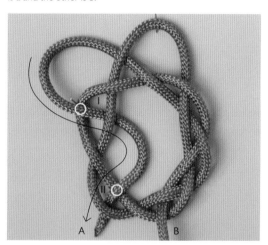

7 As shown, pull arc b slightly to the upper left over arc a. Set with pins. 2 triangles are formed. The top one is I and the bottom one is II.

8 Take cord A to the lower left, going through triangle I & II from the front.

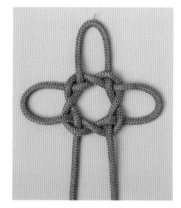

9 Pull cord A downwards. Adjust accordingly to form symmetry.

10 As shown, pull the middle outer loops on both side outwards.

11 Adjust the shape to have proper spacing while maintaining the symmetry. Done! Add a pair of tassels onto the ends. The pendant is complete.

66. *Kasaya* Knot

The *kasaya* knot is a common decorative element on the monks' robes, meaning mercy and consummation. It is a complicated knot derived from the double-coin knot.

Knot Type
Modified single knot

Suggested Materials
1 cord: 3 mm (Dia.), 120 cm (L)

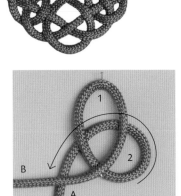

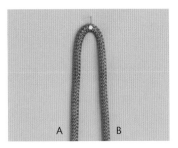

1 Pin the middle of the cord. The left side is A and the right side is B.

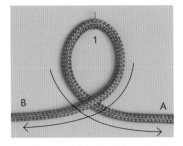

2 Move cord A to the right and cord B to the left so that cord B overlaps cord A. Loop 1 is formed.

Take cord A anticlockwise under loop 1 and cord B to form loop 2.

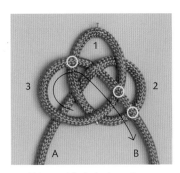

4 Take cord B clockwise, going over-under-over-over loops 1 & 2. Loop 3 is formed.

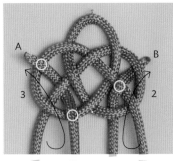

5 Bring cord A anticlockwise and up, going over-under-over loop 3. Then bring cord B clockwise, going under-over-under loop 2. Pull out both cord ends to form loops 4 & 5.

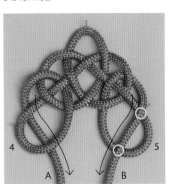

6 Take cord A anticlockwise and down, going under loop 4. Then take cord B clockwise and down, going over loop 5.

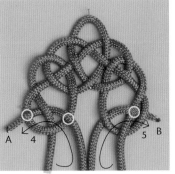
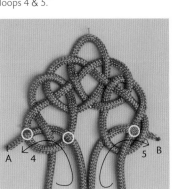

7 Bring cord A anticlockwise and up, going over-under-over loop 4. Bring cord B clockwise and up, going under-over-under loop 5. Loops 6 & 7 are formed.

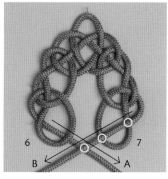

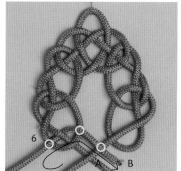

8 Take cord A to the lower right and under loop 6. Take cord B to the lower left and over loop 7 and cord A. A cross is formed in the middle.

9 Move cord B clockwise, going over-under-over loop 6 and over cord B. Loop 8 is formed.

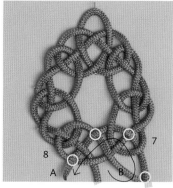

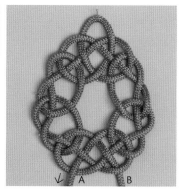

10 Move cord A anticlockwise, going over cord B and under-over-under loop 7. Then take it over-under-over loop 8. Pull out cord A. The base is set.

11 Adjust the knot to ensure it is symmetrical. The *kasaya* knot is done.

Necklace

Cord: 1 yellow cord, 3 mm (Dia.), 160 cm (L)

Findings: 1 small silver ring, 2 small silver beads

Accessory: 1 large silver bead with circular patterns

1 First is to make a *kasaya* knot. Thread the small silver ring on the cords in the opposite direction.

2 Pull both ends to shift the spacer bead towards the knot and close the loop. Thread the large silver bead with circular patterns on both cords.

3 Form a sliding knot at the cord ends. Thread the 2 small silver beads on the ends. Seal the ends with a flame to prevent the beads from sliding out. The necklace is done.

Fig. 55 These are the sublime knot charms in symmetrical design, representing harmony and perfection. From left to right: two-outer-loop double-coin knot, three-outer-loop double-coin knot, masthead knot, interaction knot, *kasaya* knot.

67. *Sakya* Knot

The *Sakya* knot is related to the spread of Buddhism in China, indicating wisdom and mercy.

Knot Type
Modified single knot

Suggested Materials
1 cord: 2.5 mm (Dia.), 60 cm (L)

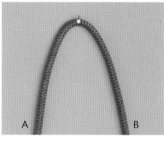

1 Pin the center of the cord. The left side is A and the right is B.

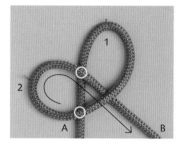

2 Take cord B to the left over cord A to form loop 1. Turn cord B clockwise, going over and under the cord to form loop 2 that overlaps loop 1.

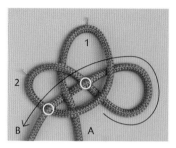

3 Move cord B to the upper right and turn it anticlockwise, going under-over-under-over the loops to form loop 3.

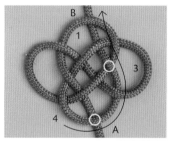

4 Take cord B to the right over cord A. Bend it upwards, going under-over-under-under the loops 3 & 1 to form loop 4.

5 Pull both ends gently to tighten the knot. Be sure the knot is symmetrical and tight. The left figure is the front of the knot and the right is the back.

Ring
Cord: 1 yellow cord, 2.5 mm (Dia.), 60 cm (L)
Tools: double-sided tape, 1 braided silk cord

1 Create a *Sakya* knot. Trim the ends to the desired ring size. Seal the ends together with a flame.

2 Wrap the joint with double-sided tape.

3 Coil a braided silk cord around the double-sided tape and secure with a flame. This is the *Sakya* ring.

68. Plafond Knot

The plafond knot is one of the basic knots. It contains a hash pattern in the middle surrounded by slashes. Due to its strong nature and beautiful shape, it is commonly used as bracelets, necklaces, and belts.

Knot Type
Basic single knot

Suggested Materials
1 cord: 2.5 mm (Dia.), 80 cm (L)

1 Pin the middle of the cord. The left side is A and the right is B. Make an overhand knot and form loop 1.

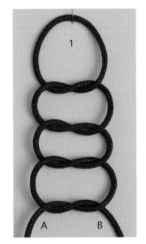

2 Repeat the steps to create 3 more overhand knots.

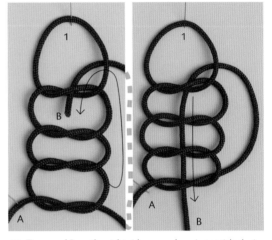

3 Turn cord B on the right side upwards, going anticlockwise under the right side of loop 1. Then pass it down through the gaps of the 4 overhand knots.

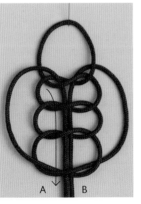

4 Turn cord A on the left side upwards, going clockwise over the left side of loop 1. Then pass it down through the gaps of the 4 overhand knots.

5 Pull both ends down gently so that the knot is not too tight.

6 Next is shaping. There are 2 loops at the bottom, one is in the front and the other is at the back. They are loops 2 & 3.

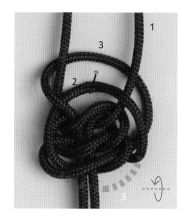

7 Bring the front loop (loop 2) upwards above the knot and over loop 1. Set with a pin.

8 Flip the back loop (loop 3) backwards above the knot and under loop 1. Set with a pin.

9 Adjust the shape again. Tighten loops 2 & 3. Now there are another 2 loops at the bottom, one is in the front and the other is at the back. They are loops 4 & 5. Enlarge them by pulling them downwards.

Bracelet
Cord: 1 red cord, 2.5 mm (Dia.), 250 cm (L)

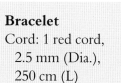

10 Bring the front loop (loop 4) upwards above the knot and over loop 1. Set with a pin.

11 Flip the back loop (loop 5) backwards above the knot and under loop 1. Set with a pin.

1 Create a button knot with a loop above. Then make a plafond knot below.

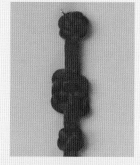

12 Let's adjust the shape again. Find the loops 4, 5, 6 & 7 around the shape. Pull loop 1 together with the ends and the 4 loops. The central hash shape would appear. Further pull loop 1 together with the ends to tighten the hatch shape in the middle.

13 Further tighten the knot by shifting the cord from the 4 outside loops to the ends. The slashes around the hash pattern are formed. The plafond knot is complete.

2 Continue to make 7 sets of button knots and plafond knots. The button knot at the end should be inserted into the top loop. Done!

69. Horizontal Plafond Knot

The horizontal plafond knot is a similar version of the plafond knot.

Knot Type
Innovative decorative knot

Suggested Materials
1 cord: 2.5 mm (Dia.), 80 cm (L)

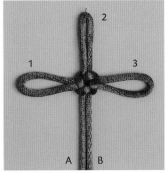

1 First is to create a sauvastika knot.

2 Elongate loop 2.

3 Bend loop 2 downwards over the cord ends and loop 1. Shift the right side of loop 2 under loop 3.

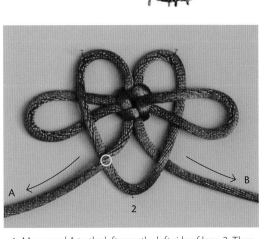

4 Move cord A to the left over the left side of loop 2. Then move cord B to the right under the right side of loop 2.

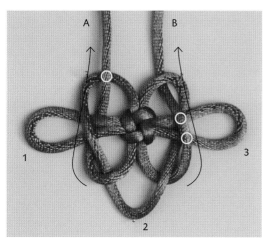

5 Take cord A upwards, going under-under-under-over loops 1 & 2. Then take cord B upwards, going over-under loops 2 & 3. Pull out the cord ends as shown.

6 Tighten the knot.

7 Adjust the size of the loops and make sure it is symmetrical. Turn the knot upside down.

Pendant

Cords: 1 pink cord, 2.5 mm (Dia.), 120 cm (L); 1 supplementary cord, 20 cm (L)
Findings: 2 cord end caps, 1 silver spacer bead
Accessories: 2 silver lotus pod charms, 1 gourd bead, 1 multicolor tassel

1 First is to make a horizontal plafond knot. Insert the supplementary cord into the bottom loop and take it through the gourd bead. Note that the bottom loop is pulled out from the bottom side of the gourd bead.

2 Thread the silver spacer bead on the bottom loop and attach the multicolor tassel to the loop. Conceal the supplementary cord and loop inside the tassel.

3 Create a double connection knot above the horizontal plafond knot.

4 Form a sliding knot at the cord ends. Attached the cord end caps and silver lotus pod charms to the ends, one set on each side. Done.

70. Seven-Loop Good-Luck Knot

The good-luck knot is one of the oldest basic knots, symbolizing prosperity. In the old days, it was commonly applied on the monks' robes and temple decorations. Nowadays, people use it for home decorations since it brings luck and peace. There are a number of variations, such as three-loop, seven-loop, and eleven-loop.

Knot Type
Basic single knot

Suggested Materials
1 cord: 2.5 mm (Dia.), 100 cm (L)

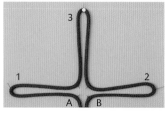

1 Pin the cord in the middle. The left side is A and the right side is B. Bend both cords A and B to form 2 horizontal loops.

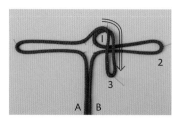

2 Bend loop 3 downwards and over loop 2 to form hole I.

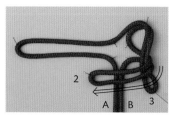

3 Bend loop 2 to the left over loop 3 and the cord ends.

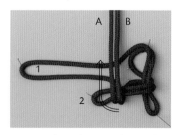

4 Bring the ends up over loops 2 & 1.

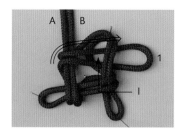

5 Take loop 1 to the right over the cord ends. Then pull it out from hole I.

6 Pull the 3 loops and the ends outwards to tighten the knot. Now loop 2 is on the left, loop 1 is on the right, loop 3 is at the bottom, and the ends are on top.

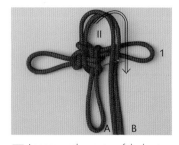

7 Loosen up the center of the knot and adjust the 3 loops so that they are identical. Bend the ends down and over loop 1 to form hole II.

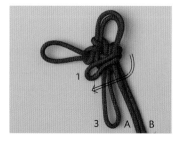

8 Take loop 1 to the lower left over the center of the knot. Set it on the left side of loop 3.

9 Bring loop 3 to the upper left over the center of the knot. The top of loop 3 now is on the right side of loop 2.

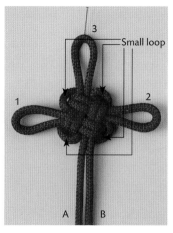

10 Bend loop 2 to the right over the center of the knot. Then pull it out from hole II. The base is set. Basically, the seven-loop good-luck knot is formed by repeating steps 1 to 6.

11 Next is shaping. Pull the 3 loops and the ends outwards to tighten the knot. 4 small loops are formed at the corners.

12 Pull out the 4 small loops at the corners and adjust accordingly. The knot is complete.

Bottle Gourd Pendant
Cord: 1 red cord, 3 mm (Dia.), 150 cm (L)
Accessory: 1 bottle gourd

1 Create a binding knot around the narrow part of the bottle gourd. In Chinese, the bottle gourd is a homonym of prosperity; thus it is a symbol of luck.

2 Next, create a button knot, a seven-loop good-luck knot, and another button knot. To prevent the good-luck knot from being distorted by the weight of the gourd, secure it with a thread of the same color as the cord.

Buddhist Prayer Bead Bracelet
Cord: 1 elastic cord, 1 mm (Dia.),
   120 cm (L)
Finding: 1 guru bead
Accessories: 15 black beads (quantity
   per desired length)

Thread the beads on the elastic cord. Take 1 cord end through the opposite site of the last bead on the other cord end. Insert the guru bead and create a seven-loop good-luck knot. The bracelet is done.

71. Three-Loop Good-Luck Knot

The three-loop good-luck knot is a small knot derived from the seven-loop good-luck knot.

Knot Type
Basic single knot

Suggested Materials
1 cord: 2.5 mm (Dia.), 80 cm (L)

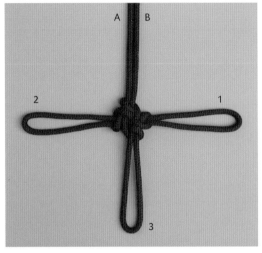

1 Follow the steps 1 to 6 of the seven-loop good-luck knot to form the knot as shown in the diagram.

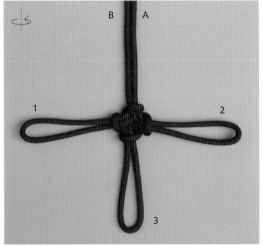

2 Flip the knot sideways. Now loop 1 is on the left and loop 2 is on the right.

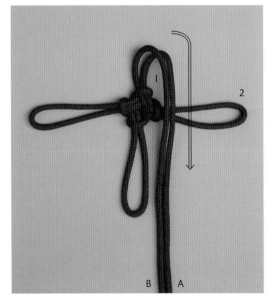

3 Bend the cord ends downwards over loop 2 to form hole 1.

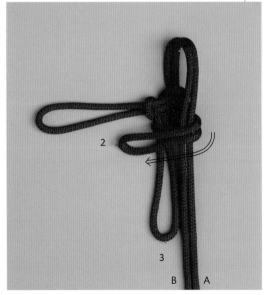

4 Take loop 2 to the left over the cord ends and loop 3.

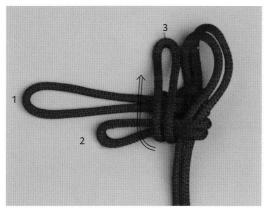

5 Fold loop 3 upwards over loops 2 & 1.

6 Take loop 1 to the right and over loop 3. Pull it out from hole I.

7 Pull the cord ends and the 3 loops to tighten the knot. Adjust the loops so that they are identical.

8 The three-loop good-luck knot is done.

Decorative Charm

Cords: 1 red cord, 2.5 mm (Dia.), 80 cm (L); 1 blue cord, 2.5 mm (Dia.), 50 cm (L); 1 purple cord, 2.5 mm (Dia.), 50 cm (L); 1 dark green cord, 2.5 mm (Dia.), 50 cm (L); 1 light green cord, 2.5 mm (Dia.), 50 cm (L)

1 First is to make 4 pineapple knots in different colors. Then create a three-loop good-luck knot with the red cord. Form a multiple overhand knot on one side, insert 2 pineapples knots and finish with another multiple overhand knot. Do the same for the other side.

2 Form 2 overhand knots, one at each end. The decorative charm is done. Attach the charm with a binding knot.

72. Eleven-Loop Good-Luck Knot

The eleven-loop good-luck knot is a variation of the good-luck knot. Owning the auspicious implication, this knot is commonly applied to decoration, clothing, and jewelry design.

Knot Type
Modified single knot

Suggested Materials
1 cord: 2.5 mm (Dia.), 130 cm (L)

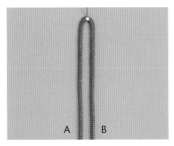

1 Pin the middle of the cord. The left side is A and the right side is B.

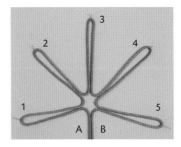

2 Make 5 identical loops as shown. Now, we have 5 loops with the cord ends at the bottom.

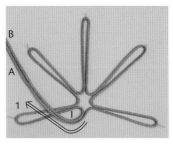

3 Bring the ends upwards over loop 1 to form hole I. Set with pins.

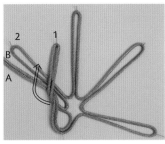

4 Take loop 1 upwards over the ends & loop 2. Set with pins.

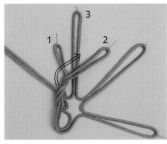

5 Move loop 2 to the right over loops 1 & 3. Set with pins.

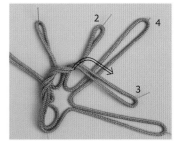

6 Take loop 3 to the right over loops 2 & 4. Set with pins.

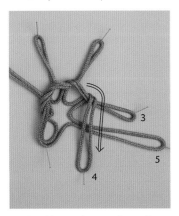

7 Bend loop 4 downwards over loops 3 & 5. Set with pins.

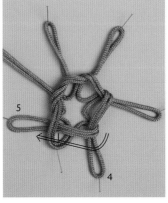

8 Take loop 5 to the left over loop 4 and pull it out from hole I. The first series of the steps is set.

9 Adjust as shown in the figure and ensure the loops are identical.

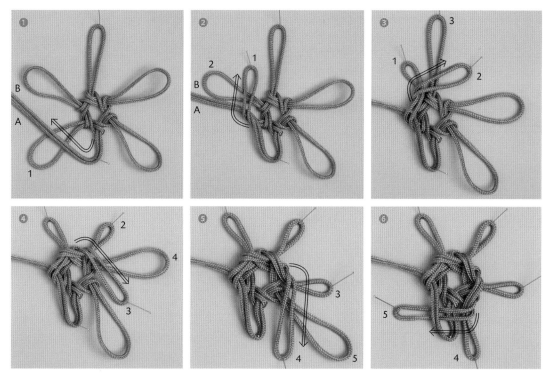

10 Next is to start the second series of the steps, which is similar to the previous one.

11 Tighten and adjust the knot as shown. Six small loops are formed at the corners.

12 Adjust the size of the loops according to your design and ensure they are identical and symmetrical. The knot is complete.

Necklace
Cord: 1 yellow cord, 2.5 mm (Dia.), 160 cm (L)
Accessory: 1 red bead

1 First is to make an eleven-loop good-luck knot. Thread the red bead on a string and attach to the knot. Create a button knot with the cord ends.

2 Trim the ends to the desired length and form a sliding knot. The necklace is done.

73. Compound Good-Luck Knot

The compound good-luck knot has two layers of loops, making the good-luck knot more attractive.

Knot Type
Innovative decorative knot

Suggested Materials
1 cord: 2.5 mm (Dia.), 180 cm (L)

1 Follow steps 1 to 6 of the seven-loop good-luck knot as shown in the figure. The following steps are a bit different: the seven-loop good-luck knot is weaved in clockwise direction, whereas the compound good-luck knot is interlaced in anticlockwise direction.

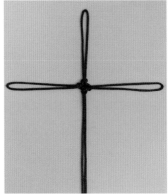

2 Elongate the 3 loops.

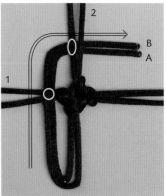

3 Move the cord ends to the right and up, going over loop 1. Then bend it 90° to the right and take it over and under loop 2.

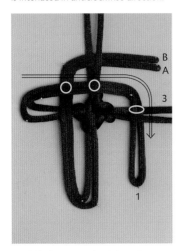

4 Take loop 1 to the right, going over the ends and loop 2. Then bend it 90° downwards, going over and under loop 3.

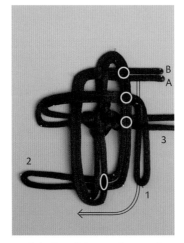

5 Bring loop 2 down, going over the cord ends and loops 1 & 3. Then take it 90° to the left, going over-under-under-under the upper part of cords A & B.

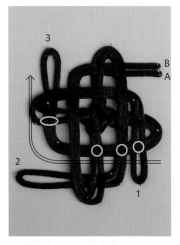

6 Take loop 3 to the left, going over loops 1 & 2 and the upper part of cords A & B. Then move it under the lower part of cords A & B. Next, bend it 90° upwards, going over-under-under-under loop 1. The base is set.

7 Pull the 3 loops and the cord ends to tighten the knot. The 2nd and the 3rd figures present the front and the back sides of the knot center.

8 Flip over the knot. Reduce the long loops and then enlarge the small loops.

9 Continue to reduce the long loops and turn them to be the inner loops. Trim the cord ends and seal them together to form the bottom inner loop. The knot is done. The left figure is the front and the right is the back.

Brooch
Cord: 1 red cord, 2.5 mm (Dia.), 180 cm (L)
Finding: 1 bar pin

1 First is to make a compound good-luck knot. Trim and seal the cord ends with a flame to enclose the inner loop.

2 Attach the bar pin with hot glue to the back of the knot. The brooch is complete.

74. Plum Blossom Knot

This knot looks like plum blossom; hence the name. In China, plum, pine, and bamboo are known as the "Three Friends of Winter," complimenting the scholars' steadfast and perseverant characters. Plum (*mei*, 梅) also sounds like eyebrow (*mei*, 眉) in Chinese. The idiom "joy appears on eyebrow" makes this knot an auspicious symbol that can be applied on gift wrapping as example.

Knot Type
Modified single knot

Suggested Materials
1 cord: 2.5 mm (Dia.), 70 cm (L)

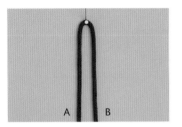

1 Pin the middle of the cord. The left side is A and the right side is B.

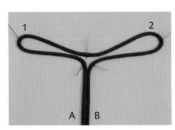

2 Create 2 loops as shown in the figure. Set with pins.

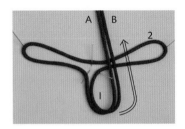

3 Take the cord ends to the right and up, going over loop 2 to form hole I.

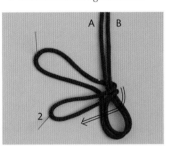

4 As shown in the figure, fold loop 2 towards the lower left. Set with pins.

5 Take loop 1 to the lower right, going over loop 2 and through hole I from the front. Set with pins.

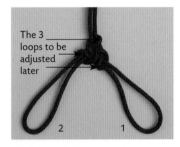

6 Pull gently the cord ends and loops 1 & 2 outwards to tighten the knot. But do not firmly tighten since the 3 loops indicated in the figure will be adjusted later.

7 Next, bend the cord ends down and over loop 1 to form hole II.

8 Take loop 1 to the upper left and over the center of the knot. Set with pins.

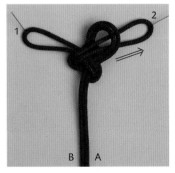

9 Take loop 2 to the upper right and over the center of the knot. Then pull it out from hole II. The base is set.

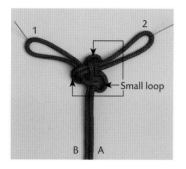

10 Next is shaping. Pull the ends and loops 1 & 2 outwards to gently tighten the knot as shown in the figure. Do not over tighten.

11 Pull out the 3 small loops and adjust so that they are identical. The plum blossom knot is complete.

Knot Button
Cords: 2 red cords, 2.5mm (Dia.), 90 cm (L)
Accessories: 2 metal beads

1 First is to make a plum blossom knot. Then thread the metal bead on the cord ends. Form a button knot at the desired length. Pull the bottom loop of the button knot towards the center by using a supplementary cord.

2 Create another plum blossom knot using the other cord. Trim the ends to the desired length and seal them with a flame to form a loop. Insert the metal bead to conceal the joint. Fasten the 2 plum blossom knots together to complete the knot button.

Fig. 56 This set of knots is made of good-luck knots and round brocade knots. Top: compound round brocade knot with beads. Middle row, from left to right: seven-loop good-luck knot, eleven-loop good-luck knot with bead, constellation knot. Bottom row, from left to right: three-loop good-luck knot, plum blossom knot button.

75. Round Brocade Knot

The round brocade knot is one of the basic knots with a very long history. In Chinese auspicious culture, this strong floral knot symbolizes prosperity and joy. Beads and charms can be added onto the center or the loops to create different kinds of ornaments. The number of loops can be arranged according to your design.

Knot Type
Basic single knot

Suggested Materials
1 cord: 2.5 mm (Dia.), 120 cm (L)

1 Pin the middle of the cord. The left side is A and the right is B.

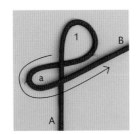

2 Take cord B to the lower left under cord A. Then bend it to the upper right over cord A. 2 loops are formed. Loop one is 1 of the five final outer loops and loop a is part of the core.

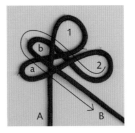

3 Turn cord B clockwise to the upper left, going under the upper part of cord B and loop 1. Bend cord B to the lower right over the cord. Loop 2 and loop b are formed.

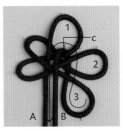

4 Bend cord B clockwise and then up, going under the upper part of cord B and loop 2. Then pull it out from loop 1. Bend cord B downwards over the cord to form loop 3 and loop c.

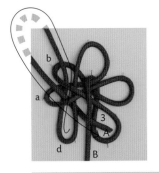

5 Let's work on cord A. Bend cord A clockwise and up, going through loops a & b. Loop d is formed at the lower left. Take cord A to the upper left and bend it anticlockwise to the lower right, going through loops a & d. Send cord end A to the center of loop 3.

6 Pass cord A through loop 3 from the front, going under cord B, and through loops d & a. This forms loop 4 and loop e.

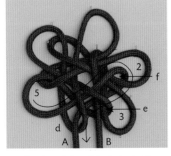

7 Bend cord A anticlockwise to the upper right, passing loops d and e from the front as shown. Send cord end A to the center of loop 2. Turn cord A to the lower left, passing loops e and d from the back as shown. Loop 5 and loop f are formed. The base is set.

8 Let's identify the 5 outer loops. Then gently tighten the knot. Adjust the size of the loops so that they are identical.

9 The round brocade knot is complete. Stretch the top loop and create 2 multiple overhand knots at the cord ends, one on each side. Attach the charm to the item by using a binding knot.

76. Compound Round Brocade Knot

After learning the techniques of making the round brocade knot, you can easily create the compound round brocade knot with a little modification.

Knot Type
Modified single knot

Suggested Materials
1 cord: 2.5 mm (Dia.), 160 cm (L)

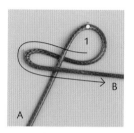

1 Pin the center of the cord. Slide cord A to the left. Take cord B to the left under cord A. Then bring it back to the right over cord A to form loop 1.

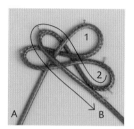

2 Bend cord B clockwise to the upper left, going under loop 1, and bring it back to the lower right, going over the loops. Loop 2 is formed.

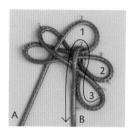

3 Curve cord B clockwise to form loop 3 below loop 2. Move it under loop 2 and pull it out from loop 1. Then take it downwards and over the loops.

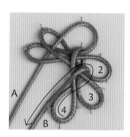

4 Bend cord B clockwise to form loop 4 next to loop 3. Take it under loop 3 and pull it out from loop 2. Bring it back to the lower left and over the loops.

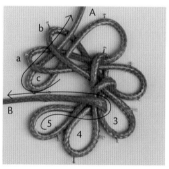

5 Curve cord B clockwise to form loop 5 next to loop 4. Take it to the right under loop 4 and pull it out from loop 3. Bring cord B back to the left and over the loops.
  Next is to work on cord A. Take cord A to the upper right, going through loops a & b to form loop c.

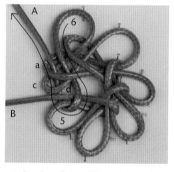

6 Bend cord A anticlockwise, passing loops a & c. Then take it over cord B and through loop 5, passing loops c & a, and pull it out from loop a. Loops d and 6 is formed.

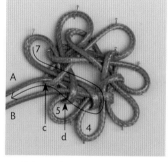

7 Take cord A anticlockwise and through loops c & d. Then take it through loop 4 from the front and under loop 5, passing loops d & c, and pull it out from loop c. Loop 7 is formed. The base is set.

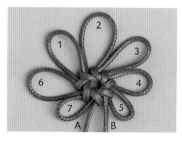

8 Tighten the knot and adjust the loops so that they are identical. The compound round brocade knot is complete. Then insert the blue bead in the middle. Trim the cord ends to the desired length and form a sliding knot. The necklace is done.

77. Constellation Knot

After you have learned how to make the round brocade knot, it is very easy to create the constellation knot by making some alternations. This knot is small and neat, commonly used as brooches and charms with other elements added in the center.

Knot Type
Basic single knot

Suggested Materials
1 cord: 3.5 cm (W), 130 cm (L)

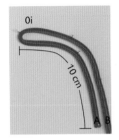

1 Pin the cord 10 cm from the left. The left side is A and the right side is B. Bend it as shown in the figure. Loop 0i is formed.

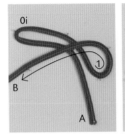

2 Take cord B anticlockwise over loop 0i to form loop 1. Then bring it back to the upper right, going under the upper part of loop 0i to form loop 1i, which is a supplementary loop of loop 1.

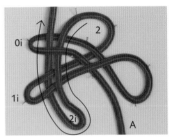

3 Take cord B anticlockwise, going through loop 0i and over loop 1i to form loop 2. Then bring cord B upwards, going under loop 1i and through loop 0i to form loop 2i.

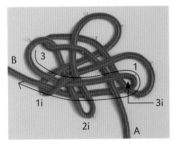

4 Move cord B anticlockwise, going through loop 1i and over loop 2i, and over cord end A. Then take it through loop 1 from the front. Bring it back under cord end A and loop 2i, passing through loop 1i from the back to from loops 3 & 3i.

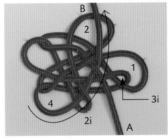

5 Take cord B anticlockwise, going through loop 2i, over loop 3i, under cord end A, over loop 1, and through loop 2 from the front. Loop 4 is formed.

6 Then move cord B to the lower left, going through loop 1, under cord end A and loop 3i. Pull it out from 2i. The base is set.

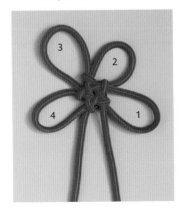

7 Identify loops 1 to 4, which are the 4 outer loops of the constellation knot. Pull them outwards together with the cord ends to tighten the knot.

8 Adjust the loops and the center to increase the volume. The constellation knot is complete. Trim the ends to form a loop of the same size. Seal the ends together with a flame. Shift the joint to the intersection to conceal it. Insert the hairpin in the center and set it with hot glue. The hairpin is done.

Fig. 57   Top left: butterfly knot charm.
Bottom left: ten accord knot charm. Top
right: traditional dragonfly knot. Middle
right: dharma-wheel knot necklace. Bottom
right: compound brocade knot charm.

78. Basic (Four-Squared) Endless Knot

The basic endless knot or the four-squared endless knot is one of the most symbolic Chinese knots.

Endless or *panchang* is one of the Eight Auspicious Symbols of Buddhism, representing the eternality of the heavens and the earths. Chinese like to hang up the endless knots at weddings, festivals and celebrations to elevate the blessed and joyful atmosphere.

The shape of the endless knot is brilliant. The composition is dense, and thus the knot is hard to be deformed. It is usually used as a single element. Sometimes, it can be combined with other supplementary decorative knots, such as butterfly knot, which represents extended prosperity. When it joins with a stone chime knot to form a double-diamond knot, it represents endless power and blooming.

More outer loops can be added to the basic endless knot to form six-squared endless knot and eight-squared endless knot. This will be discussed later.

Knot Type
Basic single knot

Suggested Materials
1 cord: 2.5 mm (Dia.), 160 cm (L)

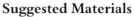
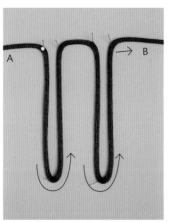

1 Set the center of the cord with a pin. Left is the cord end A and right is end B. Start with end B. As shown in the figure, bend end B to form 2 vertical narrow loops. Set with pins. Note that the loops are symmetrical and leave some space for the later steps.

2 As shown in the figure, bend end B to form a horizontal loop from right to left, going over and under the 2 vertical loops. Set with pins. Follow the same procedure, bend end B again to form another horizontal loop passing through the 2 vertical loops. Set with pins. You can find that end B uses double-cord weaving to form complete loops.

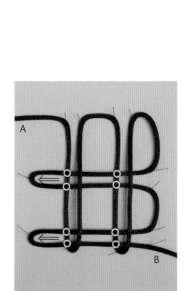

3 Next is to loop end A. As shown in the figure, bend end A towards the lower right, going over and over the 2 vertical loops from left to right. Set with pins.

4 As shown in the figure, bend end A towards lower left, going under the 2 vertical loops from right to left. Set with pins.

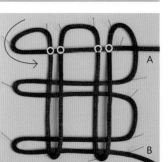
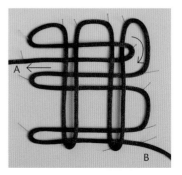

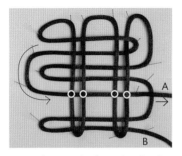
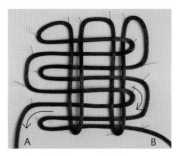
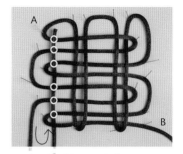

5 As shown in the figure, bend end A downwards. Leave some space between the horizontal loops. Set with pins. Continue to bend end A towards the right, going over the 2 vertical loops from left to right. Set with pins.

6 Bend end A towards left, going under the 2 vertical loops. Set with pins.

7 Bend end A towards the top, going under-over-over-over-under-over-over-over from bottom to top.

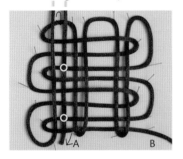

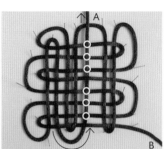

8 Pull end A upwards and bend downwards, going under-under-over-under-under-under-over-under the horizontal loops.

9 Bend end A towards top, going under-over-over-over-under-over-over-over from bottom to top.

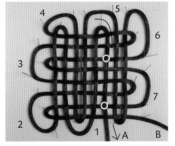
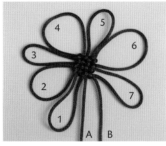

10 Pull end A upwards. Set with pins. Bend end A towards bottom, going under-under-over-under-under-under-over-under from top to bottom. You can find that end A uses single-cord weaving. In the figure are the 7 outer loops of the endless knots.

11 Start to pull the cord. Be sure to distinguish the outer loops from the center section. First is to tighten the center, then to adjust the outer loops. Pull the outer loops and the two ends (i.e. cords A and B) evenly and simultaneously when tightening the center.

12 You can follow the traditional shape of endless knot or your own design when adjusting the loops. Usually, they are symmetrical. If the loops are too long, pull towards the ends gradually to obtain proper tightness and symmetry.

Pendant
Cord: 1 red cord, 2.5mm (Dia.), 160cm (L)
Accessary: 1 red tassel

1 Form a double-connection knot at the end of the basic endless knot.

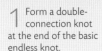

2 Add a tassel below the double-connection knot. The endless knot pendant is done. Basic endless knot is usually big enough to be an individual ornament.

79. Six-Squared Endless Knot

The six-squared endless knot is one of the traditional variation knots, developed from four-squared endless knot. Both knots share the same basic pattern. The only difference is the number of intertwining. The six-squared endless knot carries a meaning of eternity and prosperity; therefore, it is often used as a decorative item, whether by itself or with other types of knots.

Knot Type
Modified single knot

Suggested Materials
1 cord: 2.5 mm (Dia.), 240 cm (L)

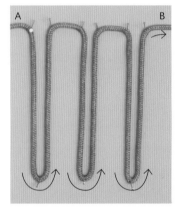

1 Pin the center of the cord. The left side is A and the right side is B. Bend cord B as shown in the figure and set with pins. Note that the U-bends have to be even and apart to prepare for the later steps.

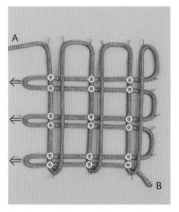

2 Form a horizontal U-bend with cord B and take it to the left, going under and over each vertical U-bends and set with pins. Repeat to form 2 more U-bends.

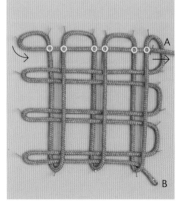

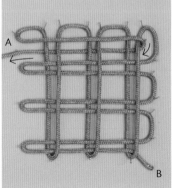

3 Take cord A to the right and over the 3 vertical U-bends. Set with pins. Bring it back to the left, going under the 3 vertical U-bends.

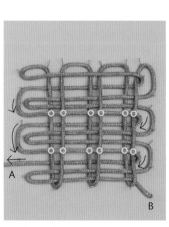

4 Repeat the previous step to form 2 horizontal U-bends. The horizontal weaving is done.

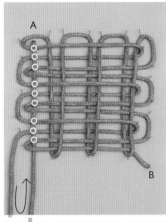

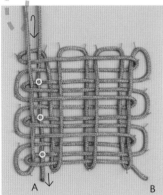

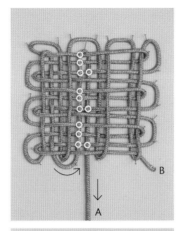

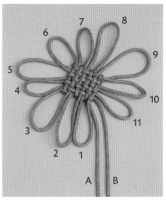

7 Pull the 11 loops and the ends outwards to tighten the knot.

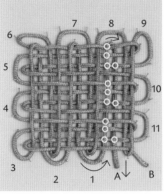

5 Next is to interlace the vertical U-bends. Take cord A upwards, going 3 times under-over-over-over the horizontal U-bends. Then bring it back down, going under-under-over, under-under-under-over, and under-under-under-over-under the U-bends.

6 Repeat the above step to create 2 more vertical U-bends. The base is set. Before shaping, identify the 11 loops as indicated in the figure.

8 Adjust the knot so that it is even and symmetrical. The size of the loops can be modified according to your design.

Decorative Charm

Cord: 1 yellow cord, 2.5 mm (Dia.), 240 cm (L)

Accessories: 1 green bead, 2 silver floral bead caps, 1 yellow tassel

1 First is to create a six-squared endless knot. Then make a button knot below. Insert the silver floral bead cap, green bead, and another silver floral bead cap. Make another button knot to set the bead and caps.

2 Attach the yellow tassel at the bottom. The charm is complete.

80. Compound Endless Knot

The compound endless knot is derived from the endless knot. Its loops can be stretched into different sizes and forms to make different elements, such as butterflies. This knot has a wide range of applications. The common ones are decorative charms and pedants.

Knot Type
Modified single knot

Suggested Materials
1 cord: 2.5 mm (Dia.), 260 cm (L)

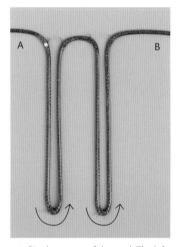

1 Pin the center of the cord. The left side is A and the right side is B. Take cord B to the right to create 2 vertical U-bends as shown in the figure.

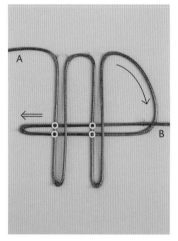

2 Move cord B to the lower right and turn it clockwise to form a horizontal U-bend. Take the U-bend to the left, going under-over-under-over the U-bends.

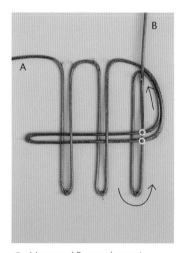

3 Move cord B up and curve it anticlockwise next to the arc formed in the previous step. Bring it down to go under the horizontal U-bend and then up to go over the horizontal U-bend.

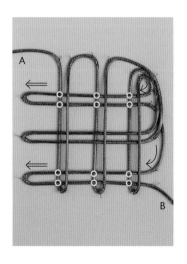

4 Curve cord B clockwise along the upper right arc. Then form a horizontal U-bend and take it to the left, going under and over each vertical U-bend. Move cord B under the 2 arcs and then downwards. Form a horizontal U-bend and take it to the left, going under and over each vertical each U-bends. Cord B is set.

5 Next is to work on cord A. Take it to the right and over the 3 vertical U-bends. Bring it back to the left, going under the 3 vertical U-bends. Repeat the previous step in the middle.

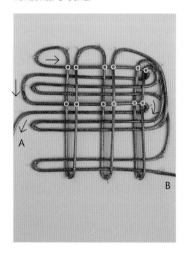

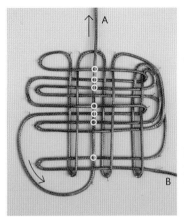
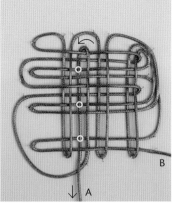

6 Turn cord A downwards and anticlockwise, going under-over, under-over-over-over, and under-over-over-over the horizontal U-bends. Then bring it back down, going under-under-over, under-under-under-over, and under-over-under the horizontal U-bends.

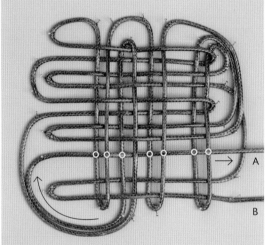
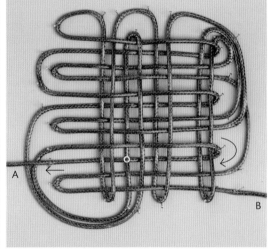

7 Curve cord A along the arc formed in the previous step and take it to the right, going over-over-over-under-over-over-over-over the vertical U-bends. Then bring it back to the left, going under-under-under-under-under-over-under-under the vertical U-bends.

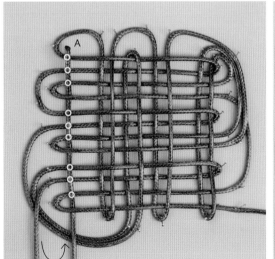
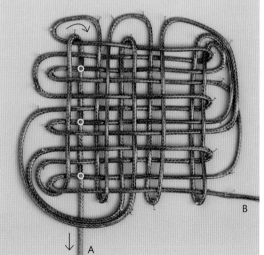

8 Curve cord A anticlockwise along lower left arc and take it upwards, going 3 times under-over-over-over the horizontal U-bends. Then bring it back down, going under-under-over, under-under-under-over, and under-under-under-over-under the horizontal U-bends.

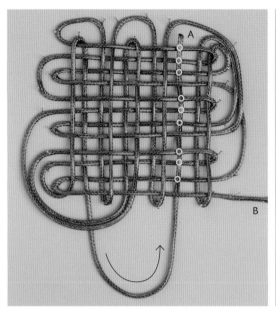
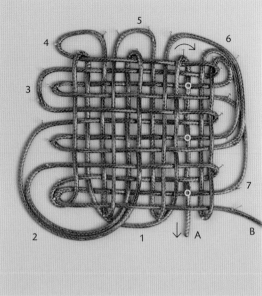

9 Take cord A to the right and up, going 3 times under-over-over-over the horizontal U-bends. Then bring it back down, going under-under-over, under-under-under-over, and under-under-under-over-under the horizontal U-bends. The base is set.

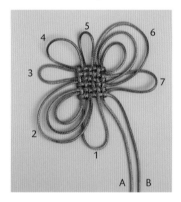

10 Compare this figure with the previous one, identify the loops and gently pull them outwards to tighten the knot. Note that loops 2 & 6 have 3 loops each.

11 Adjust the loops according to your design, traditionally in symmetrical form. The compound endless knot is done.

Decorative Charm
Cord: 1 purple waxed cord, 2.5 mm (Dia.), 260 cm
Accessories: 1 blue glass bead, 2 purple beads

1 First is to make a compound endless knot. Form a double-connection knot, thread the blue glass bead and make another double-connection knot right below. Then create a vertical cloverleaf knot and set it with a double-connection knot.

2 Form 2 figure-eight knots at the cord ends, one on each side. The distance away from the last double-connection knot should be proportional to your design. Insert the purple beads and seal the ends to the figure-eight knots with a flame. Done.

81. Eight-Squared Endless Knot

The eight horizontal and vertical weaving lines in the eight-squared endless knot denote the continuous prosperity since number eight in Chinese sounds like wealth. With the plump structure, this knot is good for making charms.

Knot Type
Modified single knot

Suggested Materials
1 cord: 2.5 mm (Dia.), 320 cm (L)

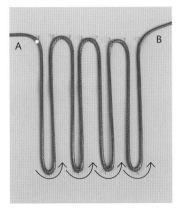

1 Pin the center of the cord. The left side is A and the right side is B. Bend cord B to form 4 vertical U-bends as shown.

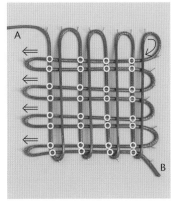

2 Curve cord B clockwise. Make 4 horizontal U-bends and take them to the left, going under and over each vertical U-bends.

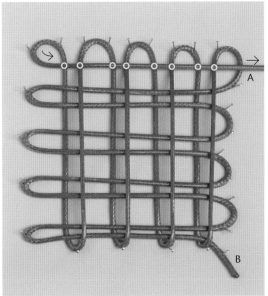

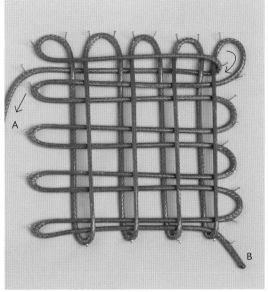

3 Let's work on cord A. Take it anticlockwise to the right over the 4 vertical U-bends and return it to the left under the U-bends.

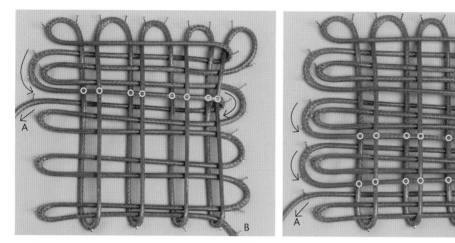

4 Repeat the above steps to create 3 more horizontal U-bends.

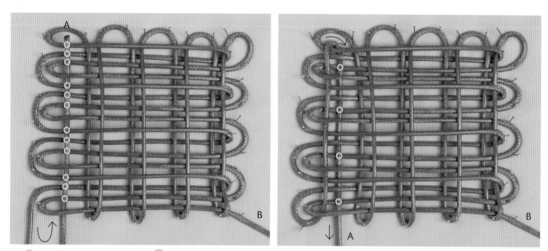

5 Take cord A down and then up, going 4 times under-over-over-over the U-bends. Then bring it back down, going under-under-over and 3 times under-under-under-over and finally under the U-bends.

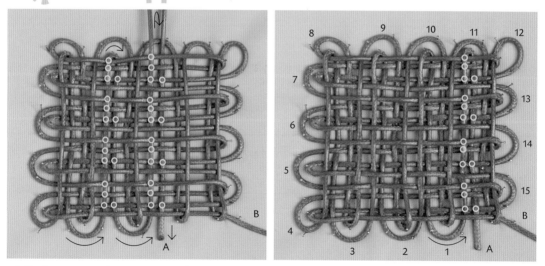

6 Continue to repeat the previous step to form the pattern as shown in the figure. The base is set. Identify the 15 loops.

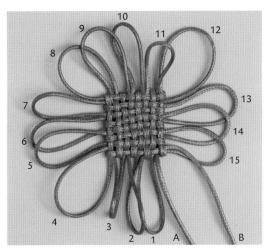

7 Pull the 15 loops and the cord ends outwards to tighten the knot.

8 Adjust the loops according to your design, traditionally symmetrical. The knot is done.

Decorative Charm

Cord: 1 blue cord,
2.5 mm (Dia.),
320 cm (L)
Accessories: 2 silver
beads, 2 blue tassels

1 First is to make an eight-squared endless knot. Then form a button knot below.

2 Thread the silver beads on the cord ends, one on each side. Then attach the tassels. The decorative charm is complete.

Fig. 58 This set of knot charms is made of different variations of endless knots. From left to right: stone chime knot, eight-squared endless knot, compound endless knot, six-squared endless knot, four-squared endless knot.

82. Rectangular Endless Knot

Compare to other endless knots, the rectangular endless knot is quite different as the loops stay close to the center of the knot. For application, this knot can be combined with other knots or simply by itself.

Knot Type
Modified single knot

Suggested Materials
1 cord: 2.5 mm (Dia.), 280 cm (L)

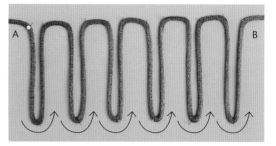

1 Pin the middle of the cord. The left side is A and the right side is B. Form 6 vertical U-bends with cord B as shown in the figure. Be sure they are evenly arranged.

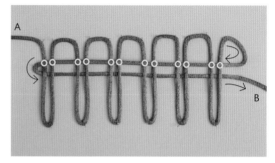

2 Curve cord B clockwise and take it to the left, going over the 6 vertical U-bends. Then bring it back to the right, going under the 6 U-bends.

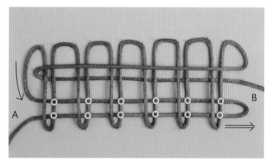

3 Curve cord A anticlockwise, form a horizontal U-bend, and take it to the right, going under and over each vertical U-bend.

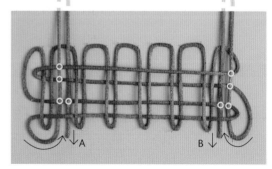

4 Take cord A anticlockwise and upwards, going under-over-over-over the U-bends. Then bring it back downwards, going under-under-over-under the U-bends. On the other side, take cord B clockwise and upwards, passing the U-bends similar to the path of cord A.

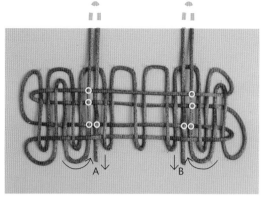

5 Repeat the above step.

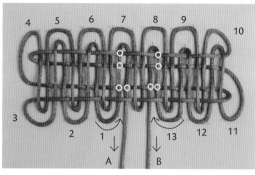

6 Repeat step 4 once more. The base is set. Identify the 13 loops.

7 Pull the 13 loops and the cord ends to tighten the knot.

8 Continue to tighten the loops so that they are close to the center. Even out the knot. Done.

Decorative Charm
Cord: 1 red cord, 3 mm (Dia.), 280 cm (L)
Accessories: 2 silver beads, 1 white porcelain bead, 1 silver fish charm

1 First is to make a button knot. Thread the silver bead, porcelain bead, another silver bead, and create 2 two-outer-loop cloverleaf knots, one on each side. Then make a double-connection knot to secure the arrangement.

2 Create a rectangular endless knot below the double-connection knot. Attach the silver fish charm before sealing the ends. The decorative charm is complete.

83. Cross Endless Knot

The cross endless knot belongs to the family of endless knot and is basically developed from the rectangular endless knot technique. Its sturdy cross figure is very suitable for making pendants.

Knot Typev
Modified single knot

Suggested Materials
1 cord: 2 mm (Dia.), 480 cm (L)

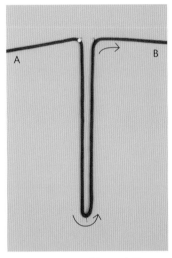

1 Pin the center of the cord. The left side is A and the right side is B. Bend the cord as shown, having a U-bend in the middle.

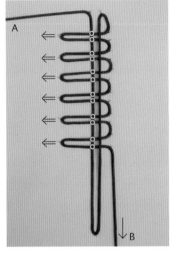

2 Take cord B downwards and form a short horizontal U-bend. Move it to the left, going under and over the middle U-bend. Repeat the same step until 6 short horizontal U-bends are formed.

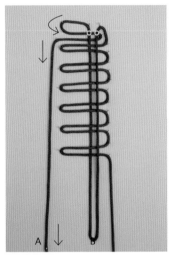

3 Move cord A to the right over the middle U-bend. Then bring it back to the left under the middle U-bend.

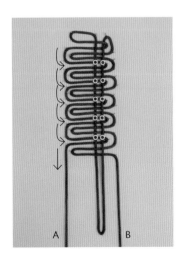

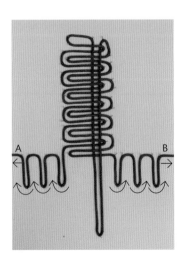

4 Repeat the previous step 5 times.

5 Take cord A to the left and cord B to the right to make 3 short U-bends on each side as shown.

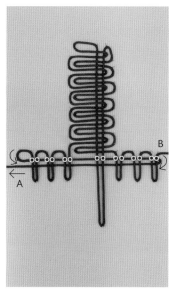

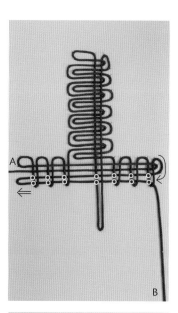

6 Bend cord A downwards and take it to the right over all the vertical U-bends. Then bring it back to the left under all the vertical U-bends.

7 Turn cord B downwards and form a long horizontal U-bend. Shift it to the left, going 7 times under and over all the vertical U-bends.

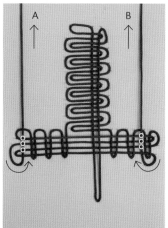

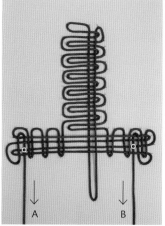

8 Bend cord A anticlockwise and upwards, going under-over-over-over the loops. Take cord B clockwise and upwards, going under-over-over-over the loops.

9 Then bring cord A back down, going under-under-over-under the loops. Then bring cord B back down, going under-under-over-under the loops.

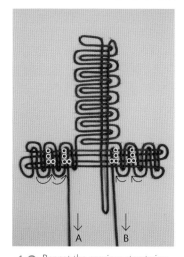

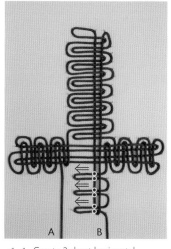

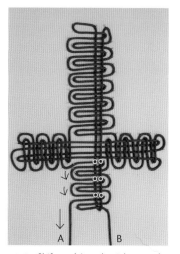

10 Repeat the previous step twice on each side.

11 Create 3 short horizontal U-bends with cord B and take them under and over the long vertical U-bend in the middle.

12 Shift cord A to the right over the middle long U-bend and return it to the left under the U-bend. Repeat to make 2 more horizontal U-bends.

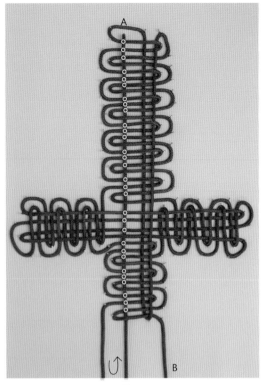

13 Take cord A anticlockwise and upwards, going 10 times under-over-over-over the horizontal U-bends.

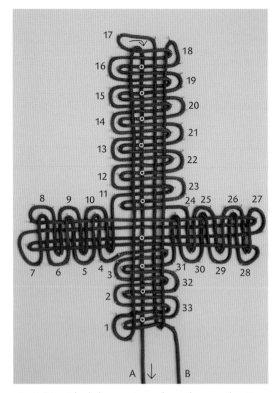

14 Bring it back down, going under-under-over, then 9 times under-under-under-over, and finally under the U-bends. The base of the cross endless knot is set.

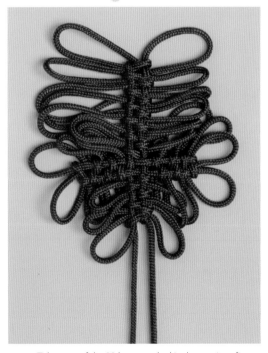

15 Take note of the 33 loops marked in the previous figure. Gently pull both ends to tighten the knot.

16 Same as the rectangular endless knot, tighten and adjust all the loops to form a neat and symmetrical cross knot. Then turn it upside down and form a double-connection knot to secure the pendant.

84. Stone Chime Knot

The stone chime knot is very popular in Chinese knotting. Chime, a musical instrument often used in ceremony, sounds like celebration (*qing*) in Chinese; thus this knot is an auspicious symbol. The weaving technique is similar to the endless knot since the stone chime knot is a variation of rectangular endless knot.

Knot Type
Modified single knot

Suggested Materials
1 cord: 2.5 mm (Dia.), 300 cm (L)

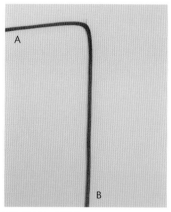

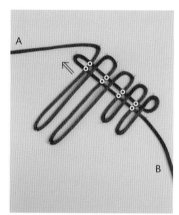

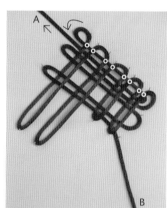

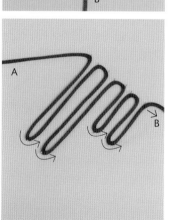

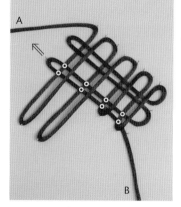

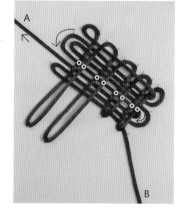

1 Pin the cord on the mat. The left side is A and the right is B. Bend cord B as shown in the figure to form 2 long and 2 short U-bends with the openings facing upper right.

2 Loop cord B to form 2 U-bends with the openings facing lower right. Move them 4 times under and over the other U-bends.

3 Let's work on cord A. Take it to the lower right over the U-bends 4 times. Then bring it back up under the U-bends 4 times. Repeat the step one more time.

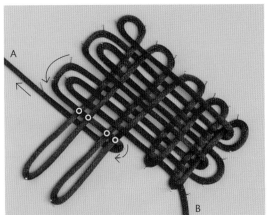 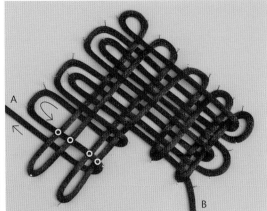

4 Take cord A to the lower left and then lower right, going over the 2 long U-bends. Bring it back to the upper left under the 2 long U-bends. Repeat the step one more time.

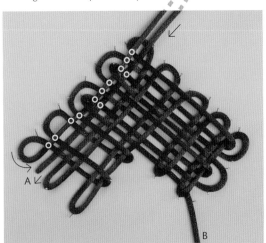 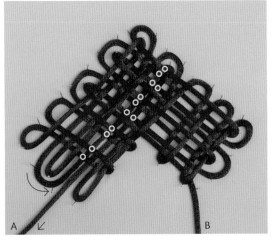

5 Bend cord A anticlockwise to the upper right, going 4 times over, and twice under-over-over-over the U-bends. Return it to the lower left, going under-under-over-under-under-under-over, and then 5 times under the U-bends. Repeat the same step one more time.

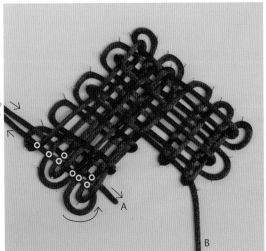 

6 Take cord A to the upper left, going twice under-over-over-over the U-bends. Return it to the lower right, going under-under-over-under-under-under-over-under the U-bends. Repeat the step once more.

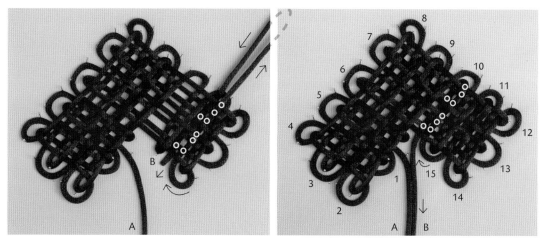

7 Take cord B to the upper right, going twice under-over-over-over the U-bends. Return it to the lower left, going under-under-over-under-under-under-over-under the U-bends. Repeat the step once more. The base of the stone chime knot is done.

8 Identify all the outer loops as indicated in the figure. Gently tighten the knot by pulling the loops and the ends together. Adjust symmetrically and per your design.

Decorative Charm

Cord: 1 red cord, 2.5 mm (Dia.), 300 cm (L)

Accessories: 2 silver bells, 1 silver charm with spiral pattern, 2 fish charms

1 First is to create a stone chime knot. Close it with a double-connection knot, a silver charm with spiral pattern, and another double-connection knot.

2 Trim the ends to the desired length. Thread a silver fish charm and secure with an overhand knot on each cord end.

3 Attach 2 silver bells to the side outer loops. The decorative charm is complete.

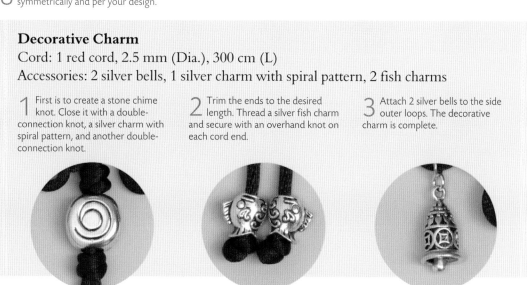

85. Ten Accord Knot

The ten accord knot is an integration of five double-coin knots, representing perfect and prosperous. It has a wide range of applications, such as charms and coasters.

Knot Type
Modified single knot

Suggested Materials
1 cord: 2.5 mm (Dia.), 120 cm (L)

1 First is to make a double-coin knot.

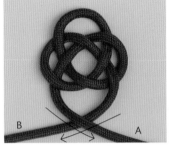

2 Cross the cord ends having cord A over cord B.

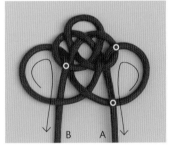

3 Bend cord B clockwise, going under-over-under to form a loop. Likewise, turn cord A anticlockwise, going over-under-over to form another loop.

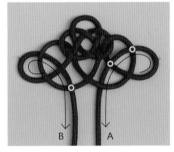

4 Rotate cord B clockwise, going under-under-over to form a loop. On the other side, turn cord A anticlockwise, going over-over-under to form another loop.

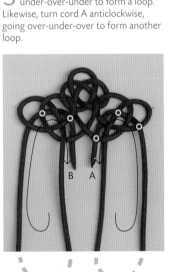

5 Bend cord B clockwise, going under-over-under-over-under to form a loop. Likewise, rotate cord A anticlockwise, going over-under-over-under-over to form another loop.

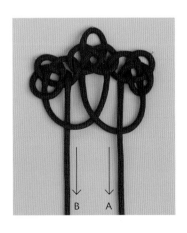

6 Two double-coin knots are formed. Adjust the 3 double-coin knots so that they are identical.

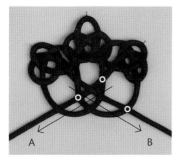

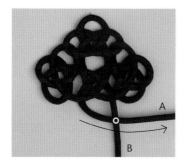

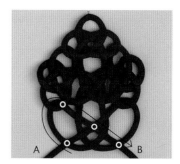

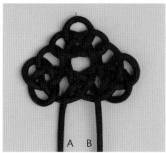

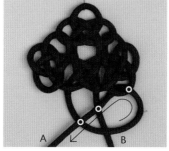

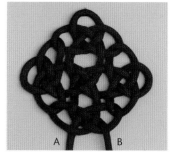

7 Take cord A to the lower left, going over-over-under the bottom big loops. Move cord B to the lower right, going under-over-under-over the loops. The 4th double-coin knot is formed.

8 Shift cord A to the right over cord B, going anticlockwise over-under-over-over to form a loop.

9 Take cord B to the left over cord A, going clockwise 3 times under and over to form another loop. The 5th double-coin knot is formed at the bottom. Gently tighten and ajust the knot so that they are symmetrical and identical.

Keychain

Cord: 1 red cord, 3 mm (Dia.), 120 cm (L)

Finding: 1 lobster clasp key ring

Accessories: 1 ancient Chinese coin, 2 red tassels

1 First is to create a ten accord knot. Then make a double-connection knot, attach the ancient Chinese coin using a cross binding knot, and secure with another double-connection knot.

2 Fasten the 2 red tassels below the double-connection knot.

3 Attach the lobster clasp key ring to the top loop of the ten accord knot. The keychain with blessings is complete.

86. Compound Brocade Knot

The compound brocade knot is composed of 5 cloverleaf knots, meaning perfect and good luck, used for celebration and festival ornaments.

Knot Type
Modified single knot

Suggested Materials
1 cord: 2.5 mm (Dia.), 100 cm (L)

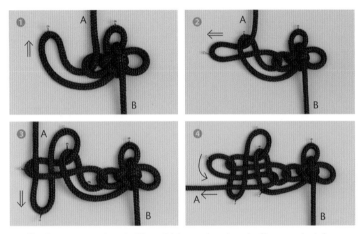

1 First is to create a cloverleaf knot. Make another cloverleaf knot on the left.

2 Form the 3rd cloverleaf knot on the right.

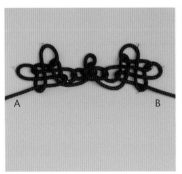 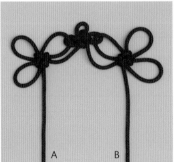 

3 Pull both cord ends to tighten the 2 side cloverleaf knots. Adjust the loops so that they are identical to the center one.

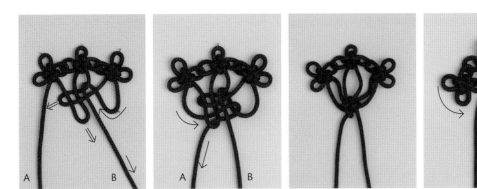

4　Next is to make the 4th cloverleaf knot at the bottom. Rotate the left and right cloverleaf knots as shown.

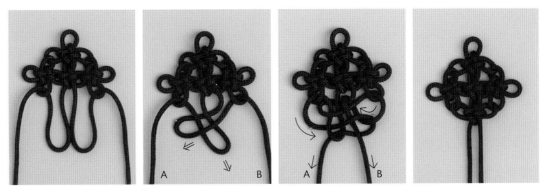

5　Create the 5th cloverleaf knot below the 4th one. Uniform all the cloverleaf knots and adjust the loops to bump up the volume.

Decorative Charm
Cord: 1 red cord, 2.5 mm (Dia.), 120 cm (L)
Accessories: 2 silver bells, 2 silver spacer beads, 1 big silver filigree charm

1　First is to create a compound brocade knot. Turn it upside down and attach the big silver filigree charm to the bottom loop.

2　Make a double-connection knot, insert the silver spacer bead, and tie another double-connection knot above the spacer bead. Then form a cloverleaf knot and attach the 2 silver bells on the side loops. Last, tie a double-connection knot and add the other silver spacer bead. The charm is done.

87. Sauvastika Creeper Butterfly Knot

The sauvastika creeper butterfly knot is a contemporary modified combination knot, integrating 2 sauvastika creeper knots to make a butterfly. Since butterfly is a homophone of senior (*die*), this knot connotes longevity.

Knot Type
Innovative decorative knot

Suggested Materials
1 cord: 2.5 mm (Dia.), 80 cm (L)

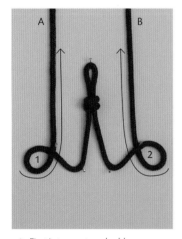

1 First is to create a double-connection knot. Split the cord ends and form loops 1 & 2 as shown in the figure.

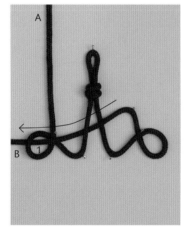

2 Take cord B to the left, going over and under the middle part, and pull it out from the back of loop 1. Move cord A to the right, going under-under-over, and pull it out from the front of loop 2. Now, the angular loops 3 & 4 are formed.

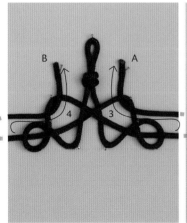

3 Take the left cord B to the right, pull it out from the front of loop 3, bring it back down and pass it through the back of loop 3. Move the right cord A to the left, pull it out from the back of loop 4, bring it back down and pass it under the upper part of cord A.

  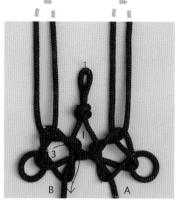

4 Pull the right cord A from the back of hole I and pass it through the bottom of loop 4 from the front. Likewise, pull the left cord B from the back of hole I and pass it through the bottom of loop 3 from the back.

5 Pull both cord ends to form loops 5 & 6. Loops 1, 2, 5 & 6 are the 4 outer loops. Pull them with the cord ends to tighten the knot.

6 Adjust the loops so that they are identical. Secure the knot with a double-connection knot. The modified butterfly knot is done.

Decorative Charm

Cord: 1 red cord, 2.5 mm (Dia.), 90 cm (L)
Finding: 1 cellphone strap
Accessories: 1 silver charm with agate inlay, 2 silver lotus charms

2 Trim the ends per your design. They can be either symmetrical or asymmetrical. Add the silver lotus charm to the cord ends and secure with overhand knots. Seal with a flame to prevent the charms from sliding out.

1 First is to create a sauvastika creeper butterfly knot. Then insert the silver charm with agate inlay and tie a double-connection knot to fix it in place.

3 Attach the cellphone strip to the top loop. The charm is complete.

88. Butterfly Knot

The butterfly knot is one of the traditional modified combination knots. It is featured by an endless knot in the center accompanied by a pair of double-coin knots, meaning everlasting love. The most popular applications are hair accessories and decorative charms.

Knot Type
Traditional modified combination knot

Suggested Materials
1 cord: 2.5 mm (Dia.), 180 cm (L)

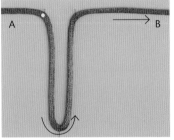 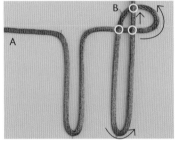

1 Create a U-bend as shown and set with pins. The left side is A and the right side is B. Turn cord B anticlockwise to form a small loop. Then bring it back up to form a long loop.

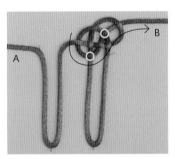 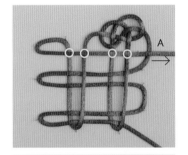 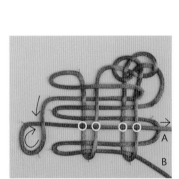

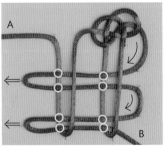 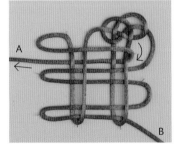 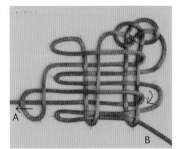

2 Bend cord B anticlockwise, going under-over-under-over-under the loops to form a double-coin knot. Make 2 horizontal U-bends with cord B as shown. Take them to the left under and over the vertical loops.

3 Turn cord A anticlockwise over the 2 vertical loops and bring it back to the left under the vertical loops. Set with pins.

4 Bend cord A 90° down and loop it clockwise. Take it to the right over the vertical loops and return it to the left under all the loops.

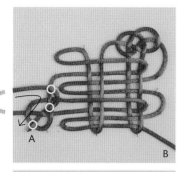

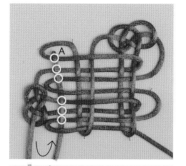

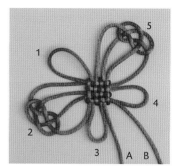

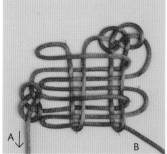

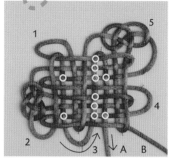

5 Curve cord A clockwise, going over-under-over-under-over the left loop to form a double-coin knot.

6 Take cord A upwards, going twice under-over-over-over the loops. Then bring it back downwards, going under-under-over-under-under-under-over-under the loops. Repeat the same step to form another U-bend. The base is set.

7 Last is shaping. Take note of the 5 loops indicated on the figure of step 6. Loops 2 & 5 are the loops of the double-coin knot. Pull the loops and cord ends to tighten the knot. Adjust it symmetrically with proper spacing to mimic a butterfly. Done.

Decorative Charm
Cord: 1 rose pink cord, 3 mm (Dia.), 180 cm (L)
Finding: 1 lobster clasp
Accessories: 2 silver fish charms

1 First is to create a butterfly knot. Trim the ends to the desired length and insert the silver fish charms.

2 Make a figure-eight knot on each end, trim, and seal with a flame. Attach the silver lobster clasp to the top loop. The charm is done.

89. Dharma-Wheel Knot

The dharma-wheel knot is one of the traditional modified combination knots, composed of a four-squared endless knot surrounded by 8 connected cloverleaf knots. It looks like one of the Buddhism Ashtamangala symbols—dharma wheel—representing the idea of endless cycle and karma. Since dharma wheel is believed to have a power of exorcising evil spirits, this knot is commonly used as a necklace pendant or decorative charm.

Knot Type
Traditional modified combination knot

Suggested Materials
1 cord: 2.5 mm (Dia.), 220 cm (L)

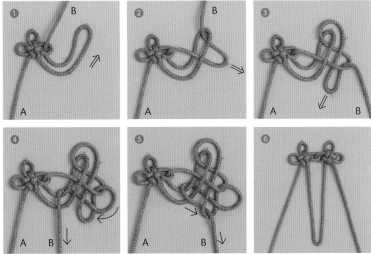

1 First is to create a cloverleaf knot.

2 Take cord B to the right and make another cloverleaf knot. Elongate the loop between the 2 knots when tightening.

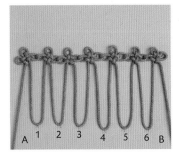

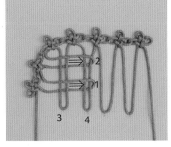

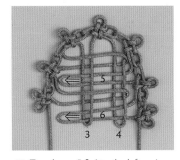

3 Repeat the same step to form a total of 7 cloverleaf knots. Stretch the loops in between and let's number them 1 to 6.

4 Turn loops 1 & 2 to the right. Then pass loops 3 & 4 twice under and over loops 1 & 2.

5 Turn loops 5 & 6 to the left, going twice under and over loops 3 & 4.

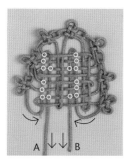

6 Take cord A upwards, going twice under-over-over-over the loops. Then bring it back downwards, going under-under-over-under-under-under-over-under the loops. Twine cord B in the same way.

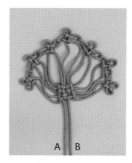

7 Pull the ends to tighten the endless knot in the center.

8 Continue to stretch the ends until the cloverleaf knots adjoin the endless knot.

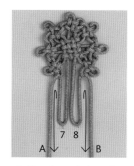

9 Pass the ends through the adjacent loops of the cloverleaf knots to form loops 7 & 8. Ensure these loops are identical.

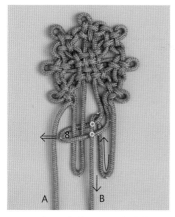

10 Then take loop 8 to the left. Pass loop 7 over and under loop 8. Turn cord B clockwise and upwards, going under and then wrapping over loop 8.

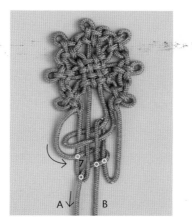

11 Take cord A to the right, going over-under-under-under the loops. Then return it back to the left, going over-over-under-over the loops. The 8th cloverleaf knot is formed. The base of the dharma-wheel knot is set.

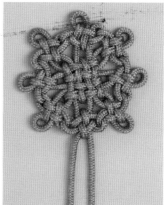

12 Tighten the last cloverleaf knot and push it upwards. Complete the dharma-wheel knot by adjusting it symmetrically.

Necklace

Cord: 1 yellow cord, 2 mm (Dia.), 250 cm (L)

Findings: 2 cord end caps

Accessories: 2 silver bells, 2 silver oval filigree charms, 1 silver cloverleaf pendant with agate inlay

1 First is to create a dharma-wheel knot. Flip it upside down. Tie a button knot on top. Attach the silver cloverleaf pendant with agate inlay to the bottom loop.

2 Create a multiple overhand knot a bit away from the button knot, add the silver oval filigree charm, and secure with a multiple overhand knot. Do the same on the other side.

3 Form a sliding knot at the cord ends. Attach the cord end caps with the silver bells to enclose the ends. The necklace is finished.

90. Traditional Dragonfly Knot

The dragonfly knot is the most widespread traditional modified combination knot. It consists of button knot, cloverleaf knot, and four-strand plait. Due to its durability and attractiveness, the dragon knot is commonly applied on brooches, necklaces, scarves, hats, and bags.

Knot Type
Traditional modified combination knot

Suggested Materials
2 cords: 2 mm (Dia.), 120 cm (L)

1 Stack the 2 cord to form a button knot. Conceal the top loop by pulling it downwards with a supplementary cord.

2 Next is to create a cloverleaf knot. Enlarge the side loops and separate them to be the 4 wings.

3 Form a four-strand plait with the 4 ends to be the body of the dragonfly.

4 Tie an overhand knot to secure the plait.

5 The left figure presents the back side of the plait, while the middle presents the front. Trim the ends. The dragon fly knot is finished.

Brooch
Cords: 2 pink waxed cords, 1.5 mm (Dia.), 120 cm (L)
Finding: 1 safety pin

1 First is to make a dragonfly knot. Trim the ends and seal with a flame.

2 Attach a safety pin between the wings to make a brooch.

Fig. 59 Different variations and combinations integrated with the techniques of supplementary cording, simultaneous double knotting, and beading can transform simple Chinese knots to necklaces, bracelets, and other decorative elements.

CHAPTER FIVE
VARIATIONS, COMBINATIONS AND DESIGN

In traditional arts and crafts, knotting was mainly performed as a supplementary component in ornament making. This concept, however, has been reformed. Nowadays Chinese knots have been elevated to the mainstream. After learning the basic techniques of Chinese knotting, it is time to apply them to your everyday life in different combinations with your creativity.

For instance, you can choose several basic knots and arrange them together to create a new craft with a meaningful implication. You can also mimic an object with an auspicious significance. Another suggestion is to incorporate various findings and accessories to embellish a knot.

When creating a new Chinese knot, first is to fully comprehend the basic techniques. Then be proficient in connection skills, finding selections, color and material combinations. In this chapter, we will go through these popular techniques in details.

1. Beading

Beading is a traditional practice to decorate Chinese knots. This makes a simple knot more interesting and attractive. Below are the four main types:

Spacer Beads

As stated on the name, a spacer bead is used to set space between single knots to emphasize the knot design. The shape of the bead is in a ring form.

Design Study: This earring is composed of 3 red pineapple knots and 2 silver spacer beads, meaning continuous prosperity.

Instructions: Insert the knots and beads onto an earring hook in the order as shown.

Design Study: This earring is formed by 5 simple button knots, 4 silver spacer beads, and a butterfly charm, meaning love and destiny. There is an interesting contrast between the sparkling beads and matte knots.

Instructions: First is to make 5 simple button knots. Set the spacer beads between the knots. Thread the butterfly charm on the cord ends. Then mount a ribbon clamp on the ends and attach an earring hook with a jump ring.

This method is usually applied on the single knots. First is to decide a position for the spacer bead. Then thread it on the cord during knotting. There are various bead shapes, such as round, flat, and irregular.

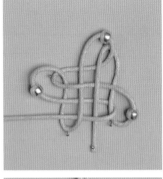

Design Study: This earring is arranged with a cloverleaf knot, 3 round beads, and a silver endless knot charm, meaning everlasting luck.

Instructions: Add the beads on the loops when forming the cloverleaf knot. Adjust the knot and thread the silver endless knot charm on the cord. Then mount a ribbon clamp on the ends and attach an earring hook with a jump ring.

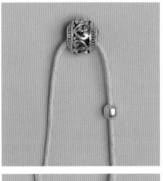
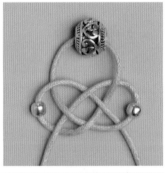

Design Study: This earring is composed of a double-coin knot, a large silver bead, and 2 small round beads. The double-coin knot is a symbol of money and the beads connote rolling. When they combine together, it represents rolling in money.

Instructions: Thread the large silver bead on the center of the cord and secure on the mat. Add the small beads, one on each side. Then create a vertical double-coin knot. Adjust the knot to the desired form and make a double-connection knot. Mount a ribbon clamp at the ends and attach an earring hook with a jump ring.

Beads on Loops

Design Study: This earring is a combination of a seven-loop good-luck knot, a large patterned silver bead, and 3 small round silver beads, used to deliver luck.

Instructions: Thread the 3 small round silver beads on the large loops of the good-luck knot. Adjust the knot. Add the patterned silver bead on the cord ends and secure with a double-connection knot. Mount the ribbon clamp on the ends and attach the earring hook with a jump ring.

Beads at Cord Ends

This method can elaborate a knotting design by using your imagination.

Design Study: This earring is arranged by 3 strands of colorful beads, a cloverleaf knot and a spacer bead, showing a lot of energy. The cloverleaf knot is a symbol of luck, whereas the strand of beads (*chang zhu*) sounds like lasting. This combination connotes everlasting luck.

Instructions: Double the cloverleaf knot and add the spacer bead at the cord ends. Mount a ribbon clamp on top and attach an earring hook with a jump ring. Next is to form the strands of beads. Cut the cord to the desired length. Thread the colorful beads on both sides of the cord and finish with multiple overhand knots. Repeat the same step to create 2 more strands. Tie them to the bottom loop of the cloverleaf knot using binding knots.

Beads between Knots

This is often arranged in extended knotting.

Design Study: This elegant bracelet is formed by a four-strand plait, 3 glass beads and 4 silver spacer beads in a harmonized combination.

Instructions: First is to form a four-strand plait. Then insert the 3 glass beads on the plait with spacer beads in between. Finally, attach the clasps to the cord ends.

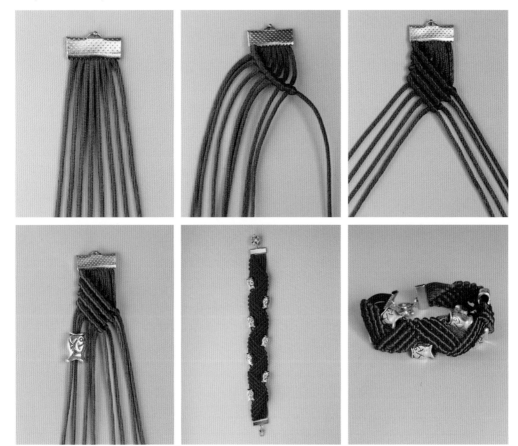

Design Study: This bracelet is a wave-patterned clove hitch with 7 white copper fish charms. Seven in Buddhism is a lucky number. Fish and water together represent wealth. Hence, this bracelet is prosperity charm.

Instructions: Seal the 8 cord ends together with a flame. Attach a ribbon clamp to conceal the ends. Refer to the application instructions of clove hitch, create 8 sets, total 32 rows of clove hitches. Remember to insert the fish charm onto the outer 2 cords as shown. Last, trim the ends, seal them together with a flame, cover with a ribbon clamp, and attach a pair of bracelet clasps.

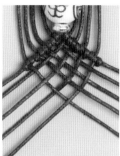

Design Study: This bracelet is constructed with matte waxed cords weaved in diamond and curved patterns. The blue and white porcelain beads with the silver spacer beads provide a fresh and stylish look.

Instructions: Align the 10 cords in a row, seal them together with a flame, and mount a ribbon clamp to conceal the ends. Take the 1st cord from the left to the right over the 2nd to 5th cords to form the 1st set of clove hitches. Then take the 1st cord from the right to the left over the 2nd to 5th cords to form the 2nd set of clove hitches. These 2 sets are to be symmetrical. Insert the 2 silver spacer beads with the blue and white porcelain bead in the middle. Separate the middle cords and place them over the other cords on the side, see figure 3. Create 2 symmetrical sets of clove hitches.

Twine the middle 8 cords to form a diamond shape as shown in figure 4. Shift the 1st left cord to the right over 4 cords to form a set of clove hitches. Then shift the 1st right cord to the left over 4 cords to form another set of symmetrical clove hitches. This is a diamond clove hitch, see figure 5. Repeat the same steps to make 4 diamond clove hitches with blue and white beads and silver spacer beads. Last, trim the ends, seal them together with a flame and a ribbon clamp. Fasten them with a pair of bracelet clasps.

Fig. 60   Colorful stylish Chinese knot bracelets.

2. Simultaneous Double Knotting

The simultaneous double knotting is a technique of interlacing two parallel cords together as one. This creates a more elaborated and distinct knot.

There are several cord combinations to construct double knots: same material and color, same material with different colors, and different materials and colors.

Cords of Same Material and Different Colors

Using different color combinations to provide pronounced contrast and refreshing look.

Design Study: This necklace is an integration of red and white cords of the same material, being twined simultaneously.

Instructions: First is to create a double-coin knot in the middle. Form a two-strand plait, thread a red pineapple knot, and tie a series of snake knots. Do the same on the other side. Last, make a sliding knot at the cord ends.

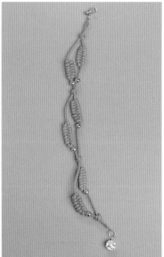

Design Study: Using 2 cords of the same material but different colors, green and sand, can produce a natural and fresh bracelet. Meanwhile, the silver beads added in the middle generate energy.

Instructions: In the previous study, the selected 2 cords are running concurrently. This bracelet, however, is constructed differently. First is to secure the cord ends together using a ribbon clamp. Then create a double-connection knot. Make 2 figure-eight knots in leaf shape, one on each cord, and arrange them in staggered form. Insert 2 silver beads, one on each side. Repeat the same steps to create 2 more sets of figure-eight knots with beads. Finish the bracelet with a double-coin knot and a pair of clasps.

Cords of Same Material and Color

Using two cords of same material can make the knot sturdier.

Design Study: This bracelet is a craft of extended vertical double-coin knot using 2 identical cords, carrying an auspicious sign of continuous growth in wealth.

Instructions: Thread a silver patterned bead on the center of the double cord and form a series of vertical double-coin knots to a desired length. Add another silver patterned bead to the ends and join the ends together to form the last loop. Attach a pair of bracelet clasps to complete this bracelet.

Cords of Different Materials and Colors

This technique can elaborate the knotting design to make it more attractive.

Design Study: This earring is a combination of a double seven-loop good-luck knot and silver fish charms, meaning plenty of luck since fish (*yu*) in Chinese is a homophone of surplus. The cord selections are glossy silver and lucky red, which produce an elegant piece of art.

Instructions: First is to create a seven-loop good-luck knot with 2 silver beads on the left and right loops. Add a bead with a jump ring on the top loop. Tie a double button knot below to secure the good-luck knot. Thread 4 silver fish charms at the cord ends and finish them with figure-eight knots. Attach an earring hook with a jump ring on top to complete the earring.

3. Supplementary Cording

The supplementary cording is a technique of incorporating additional cord onto a knot along the original path. The types are parallel, three-dimensional, sectional, and exterior supplementary cording. When practicing supplementary cording, do not forget the color and material selections in order to maintain the balance.

Parallel Supplementary Cording

Using the primary knot as a core, add another cord along the same path. Integrate more cords per your design as long as the cords are parallel to each other.

Design Study: The core of this brooch is a red double-coin knot. The supplementary gold and blue cords brighten and plump up the overall composition.

Instructions: First is to make a red double-coin knot. Then incorporate the gold cord in inverse direction of the original path, weaving from left to right. Do the same for the blue cord.

Three-Dimensional Supplementary Cording

The first step of this method is the same as the parallel supplementary cording, integrating additional cords onto a flat knot. When tweaking the knot into a three-dimensional shape, keep pulling the cords to tighten the knot. For reference, see five-loop pineapple knot.

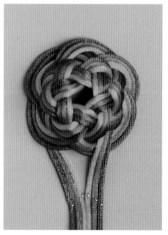  

Design Study: The core of this napkin ring is a six-loop cage knot. The red, blue, and yellow cords dress it up for a party.

Instructions: First is to make a blue six-loop cage knot as the core. Add the yellow cord along the internal side and the red cord along the external side of the knot. A three-cord six-loop cage knot is formed. Lift it up from the center, follow the five-loop pineapple knot weaving method and shape it to a cylinder by pulling the cords. Trim the ends and seal them with a flame. Conceal the joints by shifting them behind the intersections.

Sectional Supplementary Cording

Both parallel and three-dimensional supplementary cording techniques are applied to the whole knot, whereas the sectional supplementary cording is concentrated on certain areas of the knot.

Design Study: The pendant of this necklace is a six-squared endless knot, representing everlasting. The lotus and fish charms together connote "surplus year after year" since lotus (*lian*) is a homophone of continuous years (*lian nian*) and fish (*yu*) sounds like surplus.

Instructions of the Pendant: First is to make a blue six-squared endless knot that includes 3 big outer loops and 8 small outer loops. Cut a light blue cord a bit longer than the large loop. Align it to the internal side of the loop and tuck the ends inside the knot to fix it in place. Do the same for the other outer loops.

Instructions of the Necklace: After finishing the sectional supplementary cording, create a button knot and thread a silver heart bead on the cord ends in the opposite direction. Form a simple button knot on the left side, add a silver fish charm, create another simple button knot, insert a silver lotus charm, make 2 simple button knots, apply a silver leaf charm, and finish with 2 more simple button knots. Do the same on the right side. Then form a sliding knot and enclose the ends with the ribbon clamps and silver lotus charms.

Exterior Supplementary Cording

This technique does not follow the same path as the primary knot. It introduces additional cords by using other techniques, such as coiling.

Design Study: This round brocade knot is an example of exterior supplementary cording by adding a silver thread around the center of the knot to make it more elegant.

Instructions: Identify the 6 inner loops at the center of the round brocade knot. Sew a silver thread from the lower right, going under loops 1 & 2. Then pass the thread through loops 2 & 3. A silver loop is formed around loop 2. Repeat the same steps to make 5 more silver loops at the center. Do the same for the other side of the knot. Finally, enclose the last outer loop and attach a silver bead with an earring hook. The earring is complete.

Design Study: This goldfish charm combines the parallel and exterior supplementary cording techniques. The red and gold color cords are selected to amplify the joy and luck.

Instructions: First is to create an eight-squared endless knot. Turn it 90° anticlockwise. Stretch the 9 loops on the right to different sizes to mimic the fins. Next is to make the tail. Bend the upper cord end to form a big loop and tuck the end in the intersection of the knot. Likewise, conceal the lower cord end. Use the parallel supplementary cording technique to thread a gold cord following the path of the endless knot. Then apply the exterior supplementary cording technique to form 3 loops on the left side of the endless knot as the gill flaps. Last, attach a pair of wiggle eyes next to the gill flaps, a lobster clasp to the top loop, and a pair of bells to the bottom loop.

4. Consecutive Double Knotting

The consecutive double knotting is a technique based on a single cord twining along the primary knot one or more times. This tightens the knot and increases its volume.

Consecutive Double Knotting

The consecutive and simultaneous double knotting techniques look similar, but the difference is the number of cords. The former one involves one cord while the latter one incorporates two or more cords.

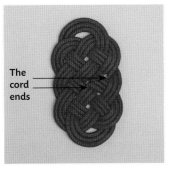

Design Study: This prosperity knot is a good example of consecutive double knotting. It can be converted to a hair pin or shoulder strap of a bag.

Instructions: First is to make a simple prosperity knot as a core. Then route the cord twice along the core to triple the knot.

Design Study: This coaster is a practical item showing the consecutive double knotting technique on a unity knot.

Instructions: Secure the cord on the mat. The left side is A and the right side is B, which is the active cord. Twine cord B by following the path as shown in the figure. The base of the unity knot is set. Next is to double the knot by taking the cord once more along the same path. This improves the structure and volume.

5. Incorporating Accessories

Chinese knots and accessories are good partners to generate innovative designs. There are a few things to be considered when implementing your creativity.

Incorporating Accessories

In the process of designing the knotting jewelry, you should consider the coordinations of accessories and knots, including configurations, materials, and colors; the knot selections and techniques; and the themes and implications of both accessories and knots.

Design Study: The six-squared endless knot is a symbol of everlasting while the bottle gourd (*hu lu*) is a homophone of prosperity and honor (*fu lu*). With the combination of cloisonné and red cords, this solemn charm does not only decorate your home but also brings blessings.

Instructions: First is to make a six-squared endless knot. Then attach the cloisonné bottle gourd charm and tassel.

Design Study: This necklace is named "all is well." It is a collection of meaningful elements: jade disc, jade beads, silver spacer beads, silver endless knot charms, *jingang* knots. Jade disc is a symbol of safe and well; jade bead connotes success; *jingang* knot offers protection; and endless knot represents everlasting. Light green and brown waxed cords in matte finish are selected to support the beauty of the jade and silver elements.

Instructions: Tie a cross binding knot with the 2 cords to secure the jade disc. Both ends are arranged symmetrically in the order of a button knot, silver spacer bead, jade bead, silver spacer bead, button knot, *jingang* knot, silver endless knot charm and two-strand plait. Trim the ends to the desired length and finish with a pair of clasps.

Design Study: This earring carries a vibrant pendant in the center. The red and silver color contrast catches everyone's eye. The lotus and fish charms connote "surplus year after year."

Instructions: First is to create binding knots around a teardrop metal loop. Next is to produce the pendant in the center. Thread a fish charm on a separate cord. Then insert a silver spacer bead, pineapple knot, silver lotus base, and silver lotus. Trim the ends and seal them together with a flame. Attach the pendant to the metal loop with a jump ring. Fasten an earring hook on top to complete the earring.

6. Extended Sliding Flat Knots

In the process of designing necklaces and bracelets, handling the cord ends is a significant procedure, not only considering the functionality but also presentation. The most popular method is the one with the capability of adjusting the sizes. The simplest way is to attach a lobster clasp with an extension chain. The other option is to create a sliding knot.

Extended Sliding Flat Knots

The extended sliding flat knots do not require findings. Below are some design studies.

Design Study: The width of the extended flat knot of this auspicious bracelet is the same as that of the alternate half hitch to provide a balance composition.

Instructions: Create a series of alternate half hitches to the desired length. Trim the ends and seal them with a flame. Mount a pair of cord end caps on the ends and fasten the light blue cords on the caps with a pair of double-connection knots.

Next is to form the extended sliding flat knots. Overlap the light blue cords and use them as the anchor cords to make the extended flat knots with the purple cord. This is the device for size adjustment. Attach a pair of cord end caps with bells to complete the bracelet.

Design Study: This bracelet illustrates two techniques—beading and forming extended sliding flat knots. The extended sliding flat knots here also serve as a balancing instrument since the decorative charms on the other side are quite heavy.

Instructions: Create a series of alternate half hitches with 2 different color cords to the desired length. Add a silver lotus charm at each hitch while twining. Insert a pair of silver flower beads onto the hitch ends. Form extended flat knots with the cord ends. Enclose each end with 2 silver patterned beads including a double-connection knot in the middle.

7. Endless Knot Variations and Combinations

The endless knot is one of the most representational knots in Chinese tradition due to its auspicious implication and the plump figure. To develop new designs, we often modify the loops and combine with other knots.

Four-Squared Endless Knot and Cloverleaf Knot Combination

This necklace is named "good luck forever" since cloverleaf knot symbolizes good-luck while endless knot connotes everlasting.

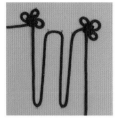

1 First is to make a cloverleaf knot at the upper left. Form 2 U-bends following the instructions of four-squared endless knot. Then create another cloverleaf knot at the upper right.

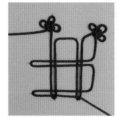

2 Continue to make the four-squared endless knot with the right cord.

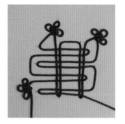

3 Twine with the left cord and create the 3rd cloverleaf knot at the lower left.

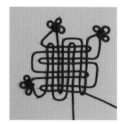

4 Continue to weave with the left cord to finish the four-squared endless knot.

5 Tighten and adjust the knot.

6 Make another cloverleaf knot at the bottom.

7 Flip the knot vertically and thread a silver bead on the cord in cross direction. Add another silver bead onto the right cord and take the cord to go through the bead once again to form a loop. Repeat the same step to have 7 beads and loops on each side.

8 Insert the cord ends into 2 silver beads in cross direction. Add a bead on each ends and secure with a flame.

9 This is the "good luck forever" necklace.

Six-Squared Endless Knot and Cloverleaf Knot Combination

This necklace is named "ever success" as six is a homophone of success.

1 The method of making the six-squared endless knot and cloverleaf knot combination is similar to the previous study. The only difference is the number of intertwining and size of the knot. Remember to set the cloverleaf knots during the process.

2 Create a double-connection knot to secure the composition. Insert a silver heart bead in cross direction and add another cord of the same type.

3 As shown in the figure, add 3 button knots with 2 silver fish beads in between.

4 Then add a silver spacer bead, four-squared endless knot, another silver spacer bead, a button knot, a silver fish bead, and 2 button knots with 1 cm apart. Do the same on the other side of the necklace.

5 Then braid a two-strand plait, mount a ribbon clamp and attach a silver lotus charm with a jump ring on each side. Overlap the plaits and form an extended sliding flat knot.

6 The "ever success" necklace is done.

8. Three-Dimensional Combination Knotting

The three-dimensional combination knotting is the latest design approach. The strong sense of creativity gains the popularity.

Round Corn Knot Combination

Arrange the round corn knot with various accessories to produce different types of ornaments.

Design Study: In Chinese culture, firecrackers are the must-have items for celebrations, such as Chinese New Year and wedding, since they are believed to have the power of exorcising evil spirits.

Instructions: First is to make several round corn knots in different colors. Attach gold decorative tapes onto the knot ends. Bundle them with a red tassel to make a cluster of firecrackers.

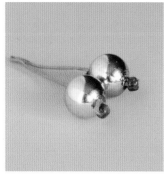

Design Study: This candy cane ornament is a combination of a round corn knot, cicada wing knot, and other accessories.

Instructions: First is to make a round corn knot with red and green cords. Mount 2 gold floral bead caps at the ends. Use green floral tape to wrap around 2 short wires. Add 2 red beads on one of the wires, 2 gold beads and 2 green beads on the other one. Push the beads towards the ends. Fold the wires in half. Then create a cicada wing knot with a gold cord. Group all the components together as shown in the figure to complete this ornament.

Pineapple and Double-Coin Knot Combination

Combine the pineapple knot and double-coin knot using the consecutive double knotting technique with your creativity to develop an innovated image knot.

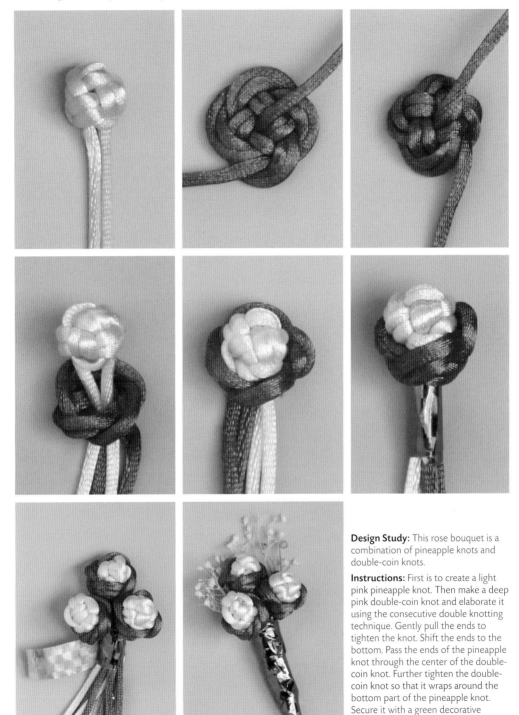

Design Study: This rose bouquet is a combination of pineapple knots and double-coin knots.

Instructions: First is to create a light pink pineapple knot. Then make a deep pink double-coin knot and elaborate it using the consecutive double knotting technique. Gently pull the ends to tighten the knot. Shift the ends to the bottom. Pass the ends of the pineapple knot through the center of the double-coin knot. Further tighten the double-coin knot so that it wraps around the bottom part of the pineapple knot. Secure it with a green decorative tape. Create 2 more roses. Add other accessories to complete the bouquet.

Button Knot and Double-Coin Knot Combination

Break with tradition and change the combination structure of the button knot and double-coin knot to create different flower shapes and styles.

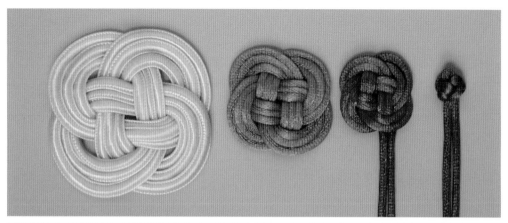

Design Study: This rose is composed of a button knot and 3 double-coin knots in different sizes.

Instructions: First is to create a red button knot as the center of the rose. Then make a red double-coin knot and double it using the consecutive double knotting technique. Form a deep pink double-coin knot and a light pink double-coin knot and then triple the knots. The lighter the color is, the bigger the knot to be. Pass the ends of the button knot through the double-coin knots from the smallest to the biggest. Tighten and adjust the rose. Add some leaves to adorn it.

APPENDICES

Dates of the Chinese Dynastie

Index of Knots

Note: the bold number represents the instruction page number of the knot.